The concluding chapters tr dominant notes in eucharistic worship, and the relevance of eucharistic worship to the daily life of the believer and the world's work.

Millions of men and women and children, in all races, among all peoples, through every range of ability and talent, have found in the faithful following of the eucharistic way the peace of God. Rich and fruitful lives, deepened and deepening understanding, true piety, a sense of meaning and a direction for living, and above all an increased awareness of God and sensitivity toward others are valuable evidence when we are considering what the Eucharist signifies in the Christian tradition and in the Christian's life.

Dr. Pittenger, a former vice-president of the Church Congress, president of the American Theological Society, and Professor of Christian Apologetics at General Theological Seminary, is well known for his many earlier books, notably *The Historic Faith and a Changing World*, also published by Oxford.

Written especially for laymen, *The Christian Sacrifice* will nevertheless be thought-provoking for clergy, who today, much more than in the past, must preach frequently on the Eucharist.

The Christian Sacrifice

The Christian Sacrifice

A STUDY OF THE EUCHARIST
IN THE LIFE OF THE CHRISTIAN CHURCH

W. Norman Pittenger, S.T.D.

GENERAL THEOLOGICAL SEMINARY, NEW YORK

NEW YORK

Oxford University Press

1951

Preface

This book is concerned with the central and characteristic action of the Body of Christ. Through the centuries, the offering of the eucharistic memorial of the passion of Christ has been the unique expression of historic Christianity. If the Christian Church is indeed the 'community that remembers Jesus,' as Dr. John Knox has so finely said, the Lord's Supper is the chief way in which this is done. And the 'remembering' is not by way of sentimental reverie, in which the Christian thinks how he 'would like to have been with him then.' It is by way of divinely invoked 're-calling' of the event of Christ, his life and his work, culminating in his passion and vindicated by his resurrection and his ascension. It is by the 'spreading forth,' or in Pauline phrase 'the shewing forth,' of the Christ as the distinctive and definitive action of God in humanity, whereby salvation is accomplished for man, 'life and immortality brought to light,' and the 'new creation' of man in Christ, which is our hope of glory, is established once for all in our midst and to eternity.

In this study we shall follow the natural development of the eucharistic 'idea.' We shall begin with a consideration of the nature of the Church in which the Eucharist occurs, and proceed to a study of the historical origins of the rite and the primary motifs exhibited in the primitive and early period of Christian history. We shall then proceed further to the more directly theological side of the Eucharist. It is not necessary for us, in this volume, to continue the strictly historical investigation beyond the primitive period and the ingredients of the eucharistic 'idea' in the early Church, since, as Dr. A. E. J. Rawlinson has justly remarked, the development was direct and in a straight line, once the initial action had been articulated into the elements of sacrifice, communion, and presence.

Furthermore, there are already excellent surveys of this continuing development, such as Dom Gregory Dix's *The Shape of the Liturgy*, concerned for the most part with the theological implications of the liturgical action; Yngve Brilioth's *Eucharistic Faith and Practice;* and, among older volumes, Darwell Stone's comprehensive *History of the Doctrine of the Holy Eucharist*. The present study is indebted particularly to these three books.

But our purpose is different. We are concerned with establishing, so far as possible, the ways in which the Eucharist can be shown to be that which the title of this book would indicate—*The Christian Sacrifice*. Hence we shall concern ourselves with the Eucharist in those aspects and elements that reflect the faith and life of the Church conceived as the living Body of Christ. Our controlling thought is that the Church, as Christ's mystical Body, continues in this world of space and time the presence and reality of incarnate and atoning Deity. In order to grasp fully the point of view here represented, the reader may profit by perusing two earlier books of the writer. One is a consideration of the theology of the Incarnation, entitled

Christ and Christian Faith; the other is a discussion of the nature and function of the Church, called *His Body the Church*. This book makes the third in a series working out the theme 'Christ, the Church, the Eucharist, and the ministry.' The writer hopes to complete a fourth work, concerned with the last of these topics, the nature of the Christian ministry. Many of the ideas found herein are defended at length in the earlier volumes, which also give the theological orientation of this study of the Eucharist.

There is one point to which reference must be made. Some readers may feel that, in the earlier chapters, too great concessions have been made to the New Testament criticism of our day which goes by the name of 'form-criticism.' The writer is not a New Testament expert; he has relied for the most part upon the advice of others. But it is his firm conviction that the most extreme New Testament scholarship, when it keeps within the limits of reason and probability, can be taken by the theologian without fear, since the Catholic faith in Christ and the Catholic belief in the significance of the Eucharist rest not on the bare record alone, but on the way in which the data, reported for us in the New Testament, gave rise (under the guidance of the Holy Spirit) to the faith and practice of the primitive Church. Hence he has sought to show that, even if extreme views are required, the historic position can still be defended.

Similarly, his insistence on the possibility that, since our Lord's *historic human* mind was limited, the full significance of Christ's words and actions may not have been known to him as Man is a recognition of the implications of the Catholic doctrine of the Incarnation, which guaran-

tees the reality of our Lord's humanity as well as the reality
of his deity. The Incarnation is not a psychological union
of God and man so much as it is a metaphysical union. Students of the late Dr. F. J. Hall will remember how strongly
he insisted on this point, and how keen he was to show (especially in his later years) that the limitations in the humanity of Jesus could be granted without falling into a mytho-
logical kenoticism, on the one hand, or a humanitarian
Christology, on the other.

It is customary to include in prefaces long lists of
names of those to whom the author is indebted. Let it be
said that the debt here is so enormous that it could not be
adequately represented in any such list. Many references
will be found in the text, but these are hardly exhaustive.
Beyond these, the writer would express his gratitude to his
colleagues on the faculty of the General Theological Seminary, to students in a seminar on this subject, and to friends
in the *Duodecim* (a theological discussion group) for the
opportunity to learn more than he himself is able properly
to assess. Most of all, he has learned something of the meaning and the nature of 'the Christian Sacrifice' from the sacrament itself. It is its own teacher, and those who seek faithfully and loyally, so far as they are able, to make it the
heart of their religious life will never be wanting in material
for their thinking. St. Thomas Aquinas says that 'in this
sacrament, our whole salvation is comprehended.' The
writer would humbly say that to him Christianity *is* 'to
make Eucharist' (in the great phrase of the early Christian
world)—all of its theology and all of its engraced spiritual-

ity flowing from, and implying, the eucharistic memorial of Christ.

If any readers are helped to enter more fully into the richness of the Christian Sacrifice, this book will have accomplished its purpose. It does not pretend to be definitive or final; it is written to point toward great truths. Less than that one could not desire; more than that one dare not hope. And all that is said is said in submission to the Christian consciousness of the Church Catholic. Into the profound wealth of its experience and the wonderful depth of its faith no one man can hope to enter more than in part.

W. NORMAN PITTENGER

Rumson, New Jersey, 1951

Contents

1. The Mystical Body of Christ, 3

2. The Eucharist in the New Testament, 27

3. The Eucharist in the Early Church, 53 –

4. The Eucharist as Action, 75

5. The Eucharist as Sacrifice, 99 –

6. The Eucharist as Communion, 122

7. The Eucharist as Presence, 139

8. The Celebration of the Eucharist, 162

9. The Eucharist in the World, 183

10. The Eucharist in the Life of the Body of Christ, 193

The Christian Sacrifice

1] *The Mystical Body of Christ*

'Circumstances alter cases.'

That is a familiar saying, the truth of which any one of us can affirm. A not dissimilar truth is that the *meaning* of a statement or a happening is determined largely, although not entirely, by the context in which it is seen and understood, the environment in which it is said or in which it takes place, the relation it bears to that which surrounds it.

We are all of us ready to concede that the effort to understand the meaning of something said by Napoleon, for example, will be successful in the measure in which that effort takes account of the circumstances in which the remark was made, the conditions of the time, the particularity of the place, the necessities of the situation in which the Emperor was involved. We are sure, too, that it is impossible to grasp the significance of a historical occurrence—as, for instance, the Battle of Austerlitz—without grasping its relationship to the contemporary scene and situation in Europe during the whole period of the Napoleonic endeavor to control the Continent.

This secular principle is equally a principle of religious interpretation. And because it is so important, we must apply it at the outset to the eucharistic action of the Christian Church, with which this book is concerned. It is

3

certainly true, that any attempt to understand the meaning of the sacrament of the Lord's Supper is bound to be so imperfect as to be untrue unless that sacrament is seen in its context in the life of the Christian Church, and unless the Christian Church itself is seen as an organic life having as its basis and ground the central historical beliefs that concern the person of Jesus Christ. If the Lord's Supper is dissociated from the Church, and if the Church is dissociated from the faith that Jesus Christ is God in human life for the salvation of men, the Lord's Supper is bound to be misinterpreted and misrepresented. To put it in the doctrinal language, the theology of the Eucharist requires for its proper statement the doctrine of the Church as the Body of Christ, and that doctrine in turn requires the doctrines of the Incarnation and the Atonement.

The word 'doctrine' has been used at this point, but the word 'dogma' would be preferable. The latter is a convenient and historically sanctioned term to describe the agreed and accepted faith of the Christian fellowship, without which that fellowship would be other than it is. Dogma is the position of the Church; it is its *raison d'être*, 'the faith once delivered to the saints' stated in minimal language, allowing for reinterpretation and restatement but essential as giving the Church its message and its purpose. The dogmas of the Incarnation and the Atonement, then, with their profound implication in the dogma that describes the Church as in very fact the Body of Christ, are the indispensable groundwork for any satisfactory statements concerning the Eucharistic Memorial—which, as we shall see in this study, is the characteristic expression and action of the Body.

Hence, it is necessary at the beginning to sketch the view of the Church which is basic to our entire enterprise, with special reference to the historical beliefs about the Lord Jesus Christ that undergird and establish the Church as being itself an essential part of Christianity. Only when we have done this can we safely proceed with an examination of the Eucharist itself, not merely in its historical development from the Last Supper 'on the night in which he was betrayed,' but also in its theological interpretation by the Christian thinkers of succeeding centuries who have sought to enter more and more deeply into the meaning of this Christian sacrament.

The Church is the Body of Christ, we have said. That is the basic assumption we must make. And, as the Body of Christ, it depends upon the reality of Jesus Christ as God incarnate in genuine and full humanity. But it depends also upon the atonement between God and man which in Jesus Christ was once for all accomplished by the will of God and by the action of God incarnate. There have been many different ways in which this atonement has been interpreted during the Christian centuries. It has often been remarked that while the Church within a few centuries came to a relatively settled view of the Incarnation, it never came to any complete unanimity regarding the *how* of the Atonement. It is equally true, however, that the Christian Church has never for one moment considered that Christianity is correctly grasped when the *fact* of the Atonement is slighted or overlooked. In this connection, there-

fore, we are not particularly interested in the various kinds
of soteriology that have been taught by theologians; we
are much concerned with the basic faith of Christians—
grounded in their experience of 'new life in Christ,'—that
in him 'God and man are reconciled' and atonement is
made.

    This reconciliation in Christ, inextricably linked
with the divine action that united humanity with Godhead,
distinctively and definitively, in Christ, explains the Christian Church as more than a society of religious-minded
persons who happen to think well of a great spiritual leader
and teacher of an earlier age. Sometimes it is said that the
Resurrection is the basic fact of Christianity. It is certainly
true that the Resurrection was the occasion for the first
full insight into the truth about our Lord. But it is also
true that the Christian view of the meaning of the Resurrection—as the Christian Church in later years came to see
it—depends upon a conviction in regard to the nature of the
One who rose from the dead. Even if this statement appears
to make the 'superstructure support the foundation,' it remains the fact. For the superstructure and the foundation
are in this instance so closely interrelated that there can be
no sharp separation between them. It was *this* Jesus, known
to the faith of the primitive Church as Messiah and later
seen as God incarnate, who rose from the dead; it was not
merely the rising from the dead of a great human Master.
    The heart and center of Christianity is the convic-
tion that God has taken action for man's salvation in the
human life of Jesus. The Christian religion is not now, nor
has it ever been, primarily an ethical code, concerned with

the behavior of men in a fashion well pleasing to God and satisfactory in regulating their relationships one with another. This is an important matter, certainly; but it is not in itself Christianity. Christianity is the faith that, in terms of the humanity of Jesus, the eternal Reality has acted on our human plane—this is the 'faith once delivered to the saints.' Anything less than this, anything other than this, may be a part of Christianity, but it is not the heart and center of the thing.

It is clear, of course, that the full-orbed faith in Jesus has grown from its beginnings in the days of his flesh. By this we mean that at first Jesus was not recognized and proclaimed in Nicene terms as 'God of God, Light of Light, Very God of Very God.' He appeared in Palestine as a Jewish prophet, proclaiming the will of God, teaching the right 'way' of observing the Jewish Torah, calling men to action for the God of their fathers, and demanding from them wholehearted dedication to that God. His gospel was the gospel of the Kingdom of God. He probably believed and taught that the Kingdom would come shortly. His task was to make ready for the coming of the Kingdom, so that they might enter into it and find there the fulfilment for which Israel longed. It is not certain, although it may be probable, that he believed himself to be the appointed Messiah, whose task, in Jewish thought, was to usher in the Kingdom of God. If he did not actually believe this about himself, it is entirely certain that the earliest believers in him, after his resurrection, did so believe. Yet even the faith in Jesus as the Messiah is not equivalent to the full faith in him as incarnate God. It is the precondition, in Jewish terms, of that belief; but we cannot force later developed ideas back into earlier undeveloped ones.

There is nothing strange, however, in the growth of belief or faith. In our ordinary experience, it is inevitably true that we see more deeply into the meaning of an event as we come to live in its light, to consider its implications, to share in its expulsive and propulsive power, and to make it our own in all its richness. *We see into the thing*, as we often put it. We do not read into it meanings that were never there; we read out of it meanings that our eyes were at first too blind to notice. Hence we see into it with deeper understanding. Our word 'insight' tells part of the story. And as more and more people come to ponder the significance of an event, the true *sense* of it becomes plain, to greater and greater degree, until at length we are ready to say with assurance, 'That's *it*; that's *what it was all about*; that's what it *means*.'

So it was with the apprehension of the person of Christ. From whatever inchoate beginnings, with whatever partial and limited understandings of his significance, the Christian community came at length to the sure conviction that here in this Man 'the Word was made flesh and dwelt among us.' Yet, from that very beginning, from those very partial ideas, it was always central to the Christian position that Jesus *himself* mattered. It was allegiance to him, devotion to his person, and in the long run unashamed worship of him as one who in some deep sense *ought* to be worshipped, that made Christianity different from Judaism. It was not Jesus the Teacher who held men's hearts and commanded their wills; it was Jesus the Lord who made all the difference. No matter what he may have thought or said about himself, of which the evidence is both confused and confusing, the historical truth is simply this: Jesus took the place of Lord to whom absolute allegiance was due. Not his teaching but Jesus himself was the center of the new religion; his teaching was important because it was *his* teaching. And, in the end, it was recognized that such a position was possible only when Jesus himself was seen as God-Man.

Furthermore, the evidence of the New Testament makes it clear that the faith in Jesus that is found in the primitive gospel is faith in him as Saviour of men. It has often been pointed out that Christianity did not convert the world to a new philosophy; it converted the world, as Dr. Nock has shown in his book, *Conversion*, from 'darkness to light,' from sin to new life in God. God, it was believed, had visited and *redeemed* his people; and whatever else redemption may have meant, it meant at least that in man's helplessness and despair, in his consciousness of his sin and his shame in being a sinner, God had in Jesus Christ 'set forth his Son to be the propitiation' and had 'reconciled us to himself.'

Once again, the process was one of growth. Jesus himself may not have said that he had come 'to give [his] life a ransom for many.' But if this is a Pauline affirmation thrown back into the days of Jesus' personal teaching, it is an affirmation that springs out of a vital religious experience and is based on a fact that cannot be doubted. The knowledge of Christ had ransomed many from their slavery to sin, bringing to them 'the glorious liberty of the children of God.' A genuine soteriology or doctrine of salvation, unformed and inchoate (like the primitive Christology or doctrine of Christ) was at the heart of the life and conviction of the Christian community as it went forth from Jerusalem into 'Judaea and Samaria, and unto the uttermost parts of the earth.' It was a religion of salvation through Christ that swept over and eventually won the Graeco-Roman world.

Christianity, in its earliest historical appearance, was not so much the religion that Jesus himself practiced—a purified and refined Judaism—as it was the religion that centered in the action of God in Jesus Christ. It is an interesting fact that in our own day, with a return among our students of the New Testament to this understanding of the nature of primitive Christianity and a parallel return by theologians to a conviction that Christianity is a 'gospel of the divine action,' there has come also a return to the belief that the Christian Church itself is a central element in the entire picture. For if Christianity were nothing but the loyal following—so far as may be—of the spiritual, religious, and moral teaching of the Master, the place of the Church could not be other than insignificant. It could hardly be more than a society or fraternity of like-minded persons, interested in the teaching of Jesus, convinced of his profound importance for our human living, and banded together to spread that interest and share that conviction. On the other hand, when Jesus is believed to be God's supreme action for the salvation of men, the Christian Church comes to be understood as the indispensable carrier of that salvation to all generations of men and to the ends of the earth, and hence as the very Body of Christ himself.

The fundamental truth that is the condition for our approach to the Christian action in worship is, therefore, that the community of Christian believers is Christ's mystical Body. It is something vastly more than and utterly different from a group of men and women united by certain similar ideas and ideals. The bond of unity in the Church is nothing less than Jesus Christ himself, as through the Holy Spirit he is active in the community of believers to make them one in him, as he is one with the Father. The Church is the Body of Christ; and a body, metaphysically understood, exists to serve as the expressive medium for a nonmaterial reality. The body finds its integration and therefore its unity in that expressive work. It is my ego or self that unites in a single system the various subordinate 'systems'—nervous, digestive, reproductive, and so on—of which my body, from an analytical, scientific point of view, is composed. It is my self that holds in one, and makes to act as one, the arms and legs, hands and feet, eyes and ears, which again, from one point of view, are separated and separate objects. The Church, in similar fashion, is knit into a unity by the fact that it is *Christ's* Body; it finds its integration in him, as his expressive medium. This is its inner life and its essential significance.

Now, as the Body of Christ, the Church is both the *reality* of and the *bearer* of the true and objective presence of the Lord Jesus Christ. It does not simply point to him, 'exalted to the heavens.' Its own interior life *is* the life of the exalted Christ. It is precisely here that the difference appears between those who follow the dichotomy between visible and invisible Church, and those who maintain what we might call the 'two-nature' view of the one Church. The former seem to hold a position that would relate the actual empirical Church of our space-time experience so loosely with the eternal reality of the Church as the indefectible Body of Christ that the empirical Church seems only an *indication* from below upward—a finger pointing to the skies. The latter or 'two-nature' position has its own dangers, certainly; it may too easily simplify the problem or lead to an uncritical predication of 'perfection' to the empirical Church. It has the merit, however, of bringing the reality of God down into the midst of the time series, not by reducing the Infinite to the sphere of limited being, but by informing the time series with a significance that is literally without limit. Nor need it imply any easy assertion of sheer perfection for the Church empirically seen. Indeed, it might be better to say that the 'two-nature' view insists that in spite of the plain facts of sin, error, and weakness found in the members of the Body here on earth, the Church itself is a lifting-up of the finite and human into the infinite and divine, 'a partaking of the divine nature.' This participation, begun in Christ's personal Incarnation, is maintained and continued in the social humanity that is his 'mystical Body the Church.' In this movement, the very presence of Christ himself is with men, here and now in his Body, available to them for their worship and demanding from them that obedient service which alone can adequately manifest worship in ways well-pleasing to him.

Admittedly, this is a 'high' view of the Church. But any other seems to be false to the New Testament picture, inadequate to the demands of Christian faith, and untrue to the facts of Christian experience. The Christian 'thing,' then, is not Christ alone. It is Christ known, apprehended, worshipped, served, followed—and, above all, Christ *lived*— in the Body of Christ; it is Christ in, through, and with his members. Their actions, in so far as they are truly informed by the Holy Spirit, are Christ's actions through them; their failures and imperfections, their sins and their selfishness, are the barriers they erect to the free functioning of Christ by means of his Church-Body in the finite temporal world.

We shall presently see how perfectly this fits in with the developed meaning of the Eucharist. For now, it may suffice to say that St. Augustine's penetrating comment that in the Eucharist the Church *receives* what it *is* can be appreciated as a paradoxical but accurate statement of the very truth we have been indicating. It is this paradox, if you will, that safeguards the eucharistic theology of traditional Catholicism from any suggestion of 'magic.' Precisely because Christ is ever present in his Body which is the Church —that is to say, is present in his members as their informing life ('for me to live *is* Christ')—precisely for this reason, it is possible, without danger of superstition or false localization, to go on to say that when the Body of Christ is gathered for its characteristic action, reproducing the act of Christ himself at the Last Supper, he is then present, in another mode but as truly present as in the days of his flesh. He is present for the purpose of effecting the benefits of his eternal sacrifice and giving to his members renewed life in that same Life which they as his members have in their innermost nature. There is no contradiction whatsoever between Christ present 'where two or three are gathered

together' as a focal point for the universal and integral
Church, and Christ present 'in, with, through, and under'
the sacramental elements of bread and wine. On the contrary, it is because of the former that the latter may be believed; it is by means of the latter that the former may be
realized in all its richness and wonder.

[The eucharistic action is central to the life of the
Church as the Body of Christ, since it is in this action that
the Church expresses itself characteristically.]As the incarnate Lord offered himself to the Father, thereby making
'a full, perfect and sufficient sacrifice, oblation and satisfaction for the sins of the whole world,' so the Church as
the mystical Body of Christ offers itself (which is to say,
Christ offers himself in and with his members) to the end
that 'the one oblation of himself once offered' on Calvary
may be made effective to successive generations of men
through 'the memorial [Christ] hath commanded us to
make.' It is in the context of this sacrificial action that the
sacramental reality of the presence of Christ, God and man,
body and soul, is brought about by the divine operation in
response to the Church's prayer. The devout member of
Christ's Body may sing *Humbly I adore thee, Deity unseen,*
as he worships Christ his Head in the sacramental presence.
But he may do this because, and only because, the Body of
Christ is revealed in the same action as the *Corpus Mysti-
cum Christi,* one with him to whom it also sings, *O Saving
Victim.*

It is to the exploration of various aspects of this
supreme Christian action and central Christian mystery that
this book is devoted. But we shall fail properly to under-

stand the eucharistic action, even in its relationship to the Church as the Body of Christ founded on the divine redemption effected through the Incarnation and the Atonement, unless we have also taken into account the fashion in which the Church (which offers the sacrifice and is nourished by the eucharistic bread) is 'formed.' This word has been set in inverted commas because it is being used in a special sense, to which we must now attend.

The Body of Christ, the Church, is no amorphous fellowship. It is *Christ's* Body, possessed of those marks or characteristics that distinguished our Lord himself in the days of his flesh. This means that it has a unity of essence that is grounded in the unity of the person of Christ himself, not in the accidental fact that it may happen to be in organizational unity. The unity of the Church, like the unity of the person of Christ, is a supernatural reality, ontologically established. It *ought* to be empirically manifested in the world of space and time; failure so to manifest it is of the nature of sin—it is wilful schism. But the Church's unity is an eternal supernatural reality that is to be realized and expressed in the world; it is not an ideal that is non-existent but is yet to be sought. From this it follows that the essential catholicity of the Church is likewise based upon its nature as the Body of Christ. Catholicity is the integral nature of the Body, Christ's Body. The achievement of an empirical catholicity, such as all Christians must desire and for which they must work and pray, is not the ideal of a Catholic Church to be wrought out by our own efforts on the fabric of our dream of an 'ecumenical society of believers.' It is a catholicity to be expressed manifestly in the world by an entrance into the present supernatural catholicity which is Christ's. Such an achievement under God will involve tremendous growth, a widening of our understanding of the gospel, and inclusion of many different kinds of witness and testimony and experience. It will be secured, however, only by self-surrender to the *given-ness* of Christ's Catholic Body, not (as seems often thought) by the seeking of some lowest common denominator of contemporary Christian groups.

The catholicity of the Church as Christ's Body is itself the manifestation of the apostolicity that pertains to the Church. That apostolicity is twofold. It means, on the one hand, that the Christian community is divinely commissioned—'as the Father hath sent me, even so send I you'; on the other hand, it means that the Church as Christ's Body is based upon and carries with it an inner and necessary 'actuality'—it is the gospel of the divine action in history, the fact of God's redemption of man through Christ, which is its secret life. The Church itself is the divinely given continuation, horizontally, of that vertical movement of God to man which it both commemorates and makes present through the ages; in the Church, Christ's Body, Christ who is God-Man, reconciles man to God.

This is the precondition for the Church's peculiar holiness, the divine selfhood or separateness that God imparts to the fellowship that is the social humanity of his eternal Son. As the Church is distinct from the world, by virtue of being the order of divine charity planted in the order of relative justice, so it must also work to conform that order of relative justice ('the world') to the order of divine charity. Being holy, it is 'set apart,' so that it may bring its unique gospel and its unique life to the whole world. This it does through the supernatural holiness of Christ himself. His uniqueness and his universality are the two necessary sides of his person, preserving the distinctive quality of his perfect manhood and yet the wide range of his work for men. Had he been unique and that alone, he would have been our despair, for no other could be like him and he would have come to 'condemn' us; had he been universally representative and that alone, he would have been so much 'one of us' that he would have been able to do nothing for us. It is precisely in his wonderful combination of uniqueness and universality that his saving work, so far as his humanity is concerned, may be found. Likewise, the Church, which is Christ's continuing Body, is holy in being unique and different from the world, and in being universally concerned with the world. Its gospel and its life are universally applicable and apprehensible.

The four traditional 'notes' of unity, holiness, catholicity, and apostolicity, familiar to every student of theology, do not exhaust the characteristics of the Christian Church. There are four others, more adequately described as 'structural forms,' which are identifying marks of the Church as the Body of Christ. These forms are (1) the Body's central position in faith, or its essential dogma; (2) its expression of that faith in worship, or its eucharistic life; (3) its maintenance and constant reproduction of the kind of human experience that elsewhere we have called 'the en-Christed life'; and (4) the ministerial articulation of the Church's persisting organic life by which a visible means has been provided for securing continuity and identity in successive ages in the realm of space-time.

We have already treated the dogmatic side of this complex; the purpose of this book is to discuss the eucharistic action of the Church in its various aspects. The life in grace, which is implied in worship and grounded in dogma, will be considered toward the close of this volume, involving, as it does, both personal growth into the likeness of Christ and the social expression of that 'en-Christedness' in every relationship. The one structure that must be mentioned here, although in nothing like sufficient detail, is the ministerial articulation of the Church's life as the Body of Christ. And this for two reasons: first, that it is not frequently enough recognized that the ministry is one of the essential structural forms of the Church; second, because recent discussion of this subject has often been misguided and, indeed, mistaken.

If the ministry is regarded as a relatively unimportant or secondary consideration, the Body of Christ tends to lose its distinctive quality as *this* kind of a body rather than some or any other kind—it becomes ill-defined and unidentifiable. On the other hand, the conception of the ministry as independent of the Church, and itself a separate channel of grace, can lead to a demonic notion of the ministry as the exclusive criterion of Christianity rather than as the inescapable expression of the Body. And if the ministry is thought to be changeable at will, without regard to historical developments, an indifference to the principle of continuity may result, with serious consequences in other areas as well as in the ministerial area. All these errors have their inevitable influence on the view of the Eucharist entertained by their proponents. One might almost say that the surest indication of the interdependence and interpenetration of the several structural forms is to be found at this point.

When the ministry is conceived of as isolated from the Church and therefore given a position of its own, existing independently of the total Body and, as it were, 'feeding grace' into the Body, the Eucharist comes to be considered a work performed by the priest *instead of* the Body rather than *on behalf of* the Body. When the ministry is thought to be relatively unimportant, or when its particular forms of expression are thought to be changeable at will, the Christian action of worship tends to lose its markedly traditional character, to become congregational in the narrowest sense, or to vary in its supposed effectiveness according to the 'worthiness' (spiritual or moral) of the chosen officiant. Hence the extraordinary importance, on all counts, of a sound view of the ministerial articulation of the Body of Christ.

Christianity emerged from the womb of the older Israel 'after the flesh,' with a faith that was inchoate and undefined, although the essence of it was clear enough. The Eucharist, as we shall see in the following chapters, began with a similar germinal stage. The theological understanding that later became normative was not reached until some time after the Resurrection and the emergence of the Christian community as a self-conscious entity. Some writers, even today, endeavor to push the later developments back into the days of our Lord's life, or at least into the first few years of the Christian Church. But it is much more likely, indeed it is certain, that in both faith and worship there was a considerable period of fluidity, during which the line of development that the Catholic centuries were to vindicate was taking shape. There is nothing wicked in this admission, nor does it constitute (for any believer in the guidance of the Holy Spirit) a criticism of the developed traditional faith and the developed traditional worship of those Catholic centuries. It is simply a fact, one of those which, as Bishop Butler said in his oft-quoted epigram, 'will be what they will be.' Hence there is no reason, as the Bishop added, to 'wish them otherwise.' Like all living things, the Christian tradition grew from certain beginnings to certain conclusions, from beginnings which were not obviously and explicitly, what later thought and experience rightly came to see in them.

It was not otherwise with the ministry of the Church. The Jewish background of that ministry is increasingly plain to us as our knowledge of the whole Judaistic period becomes more accurate. The Christian ministry came out of the Jewish Church, with its elders, its synagogue government, its rabbis and their disciples. It was not to be confined to this Jewish pattern; it did begin there. The way in which this primitive ministry, if we may call it such, grew into the threefold ministry of bishops, priests, and deacons, which it is 'the intent' of the Anglican Communion to 'continue, and reverently use and esteem,' is by no means as clear as we might wish. In any case, the conclusion of the matter is plain enough. Within two hundred years, and most probably by the middle of the second century, it was normal in every quarter of Christendom to have the bishop, who administered the Eucharist and alone ordained; the presbyters (or priests), who at this time did not normally celebrate the Eucharist but soon were delegated by the bishop for this function in the Body; and the deacons, who assisted the bishop at the celebration and served as aides in pastoral work. In another hundred years, the lines were even more plainly observed: the bishop as chief pastor and ordainer; the priest, celebrant of the mysteries in local churches where no bishop was available; the deacons, assistant ministers under the bishops.

The important point in our discussion, however, is not the way in which the ministry may or may not have developed; about that, opinion differs and will very likely continue to differ. The point is that by the end of the early period, certainly by A.D. 300, the Christian Church had developed a ministerial structure which was, despite St. Jerome's later gibes, everywhere accepted; which was as natural to Christianity as, although it achieved form before, its articulated faith, its articulated worship, and its articulated moral standards; and which, since that time, has continued to be the one duly authenticated ministry in Christendom. It is as if the new life of Christianity, after its emergence from Judaism, required some time to strike out its own distinctive line of growth. First the ministry was developed; next the worship; and finally the faith— 'developed,' that is, not by creation *de novo*, but by emerging into form from germinal beginnings. The Christian community historically came to have what we have called specific structural forms; the ministry was one of these.

But let us remember that the Church is the Body of Christ. It is not a congeries of individual Christians, but a living organism whose life is Christ and whose guiding agent is the Holy Spirit. So we must say that the ministry is not properly understood if it is thought to be an instance of expedient human planning; neither is it rightly conceived if its growth is described as accidental. It is properly understood and rightly conceived only if it is seen as a divine gift, received through the process of historical development—for how else could it be received, unless it were dropped as a bolt from the blue?—but molded by the life of the risen yet indwelling Christ as he by the Holy Spirit worked through the Holy Catholic Church as his Body upon earth. The ministry is the gift of God to his Church as the representative functioning agent for the Body.

The Church is integral to the whole complex fact of Christ, which means that it is part of the incarnate and incarnating, the atoning and redeeming, work of the eternal Word of God. If Christ is the High Priest who is mediator between God and man, the Church as his Body is possessed of the same priesthood: Christ as Priest is Lord of his Body, its Head and its informing Life. Hence the Church as Body of Christ is Priest between God and man, its priesthood not delegated to it but identical with the priesthood of its Head Christ. Christ in his Church is the giver of salvation, the mediator between God and man; the whole body of the faithful, in so far as they, by membership in Christ, share in his life, are sharers also in his priesthood. They are priests not because of any individual relationship that they sustain to God; they are such only through sharing in the one underived priesthood, which is Christ's own priesthood extended in his mystical Body. The ministerial priesthood, belonging to those who are appointed by special ordination to act for the Body of Christ, is a priesthood by Christ's own appointment and by his gift. But it is a priesthood of the Church; it is not *instead of*, but *on behalf of*, the Church's priesthood, precisely as it is not instead of but on behalf of *Christ's* priesthood, for Christ's priesthood and the Church's priesthood are identical.

The function of the episcopate in this organic society is not primarily to *govern*, although that work was given to it in the course of time. Its primary function is to act as the chief steward of the Christian gospel and sacraments, ministry and life in grace. In early days, it is very likely that much of the government was locally retained by the presbyters, after the Jewish pattern, but the bishops were always the ordaining agents, the chief sacramental ministers, the witnesses to the faith and life of Christianity. This is shown by the way in which lists of bishops were used by early writers. The bishops were the guarantors of the continuity and identity of the Church's historically given gospel, the authenticators of its sacraments, the perpetuators of its ministry, the guardians of its life.

Each office in the Church's ministry is functional for the whole Church. That is to say, it is functional for Christ himself, who alone is 'the Bishop of our souls,' the 'great High Priest,' the true 'Servant of the servants of God'; all ordination is by him and for his purposes in his

Body. This does not mean that any individual congregation or group calling itself 'a church' can set up its own functioning ministry. The only ministry that can function for the Church of Christ is the ministry of the whole Body, one that has been duly witnessed to and authenticated by the whole Body, and also 'reverently used and esteemed' by the whole Body. There is only one kind of ministry that has been rightly witnessed, authenticated, 'used and esteemed' by the whole Body; it is 'the ministry of the apostolic succession,' interpreted not mechanically or legalistically, but vitally and dynamically. Individual congregations that create their own 'ministries,' or groups calling themselves 'churches' that have set up 'ministries' different from the historical ministry of the Church, may have acted for reasons that seemed good and sound to them—indeed, for reasons that have a certain historical plausibility. That is beside the point. In so doing, they have departed from the life of the whole Church in that particular structural form that concerns its continuity and identity—namely, the ministerial articulation. Even when they thought they were reverting to some more primitive form, they were arrogating to themselves as a small group the right to do that which no group can do. They intended to modify the line of growth that the Body of Christ historically had taken, remaking the Church after their own desire, or their own reading of what might have been or should have been; and they were thereby guilty of an anachronism that denies the vital life of the Body.

Now that there is a schism in the empirical Church, a way must be found by which to reintegrate these separated groups into the tradition of historic Christianity. This must be done without a denial of what von Hügel called the 'God-given graces and mercies' that have come through the separated groups and through their particular ministries. No one would wish to deny the spiritual benefit and the genuine efficacy of these ministries, nor minimize the Christian faith and life exhibited by the groups to which they minister. But it would be untrue to the facts to pretend that there is no difference between these particular ministries and the Church's traditional ministry. The former have not been rightly authenticated, 'used and esteemed' by the whole Church, in the sense in which the latter has been established. Much good they have done and still do. As a prophetic ministry of the Word of God, they have great accomplishments to their credit. As a ministry *identical* with the traditional ministry that the Body of Christ developed in its first three centuries and has continued to authenticate since that time, they have no proper claim to make.

In our consideration of the Christian Sacrifice, on succeeding pages, we shall mean that eucharistic action which is performed on behalf of the Body of Christ by men authenticated as ministerial priests and ordained by those who have had authentic appointment from the whole Body of Christ for this very function. Lest it be thought that our view is narrow and limited, making further development in the Church impossible, let it be said flatly that it is our conviction that only with such a ministerial articulation as the Church has maintained can true development be possible. Development means change along a line already struck out by the organism, so that the organism continues to be itself even while it grows and adapts to new situations and new circumstances. Change without this 'control' is not development at all; it is sheer novelty, innovation without identity, and is likely to lead to conclusions that bear little resemblance to the original reality.

The Church is the Body of Christ. Like a body and as a body, it changes as it grows. But since it is Christ's Body, it is always recognizably the same, possessing such historical continuity and such persisting identity as will enable us to see that it is in fact itself. This has been true in the past; it must be true in the future. We recognize the Body of Christ when we hear the historic gospel of the God who 'for us men and for our salvation' lived as Jesus of Nazareth, God in human life to redeem us from sin and empower us for eternal life; when we witness the pleading of the sacrifice of Christ as the Holy Eucharist is offered; when we are conscious of the life in Christ which that faith empowers and that worship nourishes; and when we see the historic ministry, functioning responsibly in his mystical Body for the incarnate Christ who is the Saviour of the world.

2] *The Eucharist in the New Testament*

The 'genetic fallacy' has never been more plainly manifested than in much of the discussion that has centered in the Christian Eucharist. By the 'genetic fallacy' we mean the notion that the meaning and significance of a belief or rite are determined solely by its origins, so that development and growth are looked upon with grave suspicion or even dismissed as necessary and inevitable degeneration or deterioration. Perhaps it is in modern times particularly, with the appearance of what is sometimes called 'scientific history,' that the tendency toward 'geneticism' has grown apace. In any event, this fallacy is found especially in the treatment of religious questions, and among those who have investigated the origins of Christianity it is a peculiarly tempting point of view.

A number of years ago, the writer was engaged in a long and detailed analysis of Christian development, in collaboration with a distinguished historian. During the discussion of certain aspects of the matter, the historian remarked, 'It's a long way from the Sermon on the Mount to the Nicene Creed.' To which the writer replied, rather tartly, 'Yes, it's about three hundred years.' While the retort was rude, it was justified at least to this extent: the historian plainly meant to imply that the story of the development of Christian dogma concerning the person of Christ represented a continuing corruption of the simple gospel of divine love and human brotherhood, which he felt was the essence of Christianity as taught and lived by the historic Jesus of Nazareth. He believed that Christianity, in terms of what he conceived to be its original proclamation by the Nazarene, must be retained in its original form and that the subsequent development was certainly a mistake.

Now in the particular problem that was then under discussion, New Testament studies have conclusively shown that Christianity was never the simple gospel that the historian thought it to be. From its beginnings it was something quite unlike the 'eternal life in the midst of time,' with divine fatherhood and human brotherliness as its manifestations, which writers like Harnack had presented. The study of eschatology, the grasp of the way in which the gospels spring from the primitive community's life in faith, and the whole discipline of form-criticism have given us a different picture of how Christianity came to be. But quite apart from such considerations, it is not at all an impossibility that the deepest and truest meaning of Christianity, the real significance of its Founder, and the value and enduring content of the religion that is called by his name are to be discovered not in specific origins such as might conceivably be traced by some 'scientific historian' if he had all the data at his disposal; rather, we may well believe, they are to be discovered in *that which came out of* this primitive event and situation. In the previous chapter, we pointed out this important truth. And perhaps it is generally agreed that Christianity is not simply the religion taught by Jesus of Nazareth, the Teacher and Master. It is the religion that finds God at work in him, that worships God present there and that experiences reconciliation with God through the total reality of Christ's life and continuing activity. Furthermore, from our present point of view, it is the religion that is conveyed by, and is possible only within, the community of faith, which is the Body of Christ, instrumentally operative in the world as the social humanity that continues the human action of God in his Incarnation.

Yet when we turn to the central Christian rite, the tendency to fall back into 'geneticism' is present in many scholars. The so-called simple 'Last Supper,' in which a final 'meal of fellowship' was shared by Jesus with his disciples, is believed to indicate the only significance that can be given to the later Eucharist. The historical development from that simple meal is considered erroneous, even superstitious; the whole eucharistic theology of the Church in succeeding generations is regarded as a perversion of the intention of Jesus. Here, plainly, is another example of the 'genetic fallacy.' If it were true that historically the Last Supper was simply a final 'meal of fellowship,' with no obvious significance beyond that, it would not follow that it possessed that meaning *alone*, in an ultimate and determinative sense. What has *come out of* that Last Supper would be as significant for an understanding of its fundamental meaning as the supposed actions in the Upper Room on 'the night in which he was betrayed.' It is surely the testimony of any sound Christian philosophical investigation of the meaning of history that minimal statement in terms of origins is not exhaustive of the *meaning* of events. Hence it would be possible to maintain that the fully developed

Christian eucharistic rite and theology are a valid and proper expansion of that initial action in the Upper Room, as the Holy Spirit led the primitive community, later the apostolic company, and finally the early Church, to see more and more deeply what was in fact involved there. Furthermore, faith in the Incarnation would suggest that while, in his *human* mind, the historic Jesus might not have been aware of the full implications of his actions at the Last Supper, the purpose of God in the 'mind' of the Eternal Word (incarnate as Jesus) would still be operative in ordaining the Christian Sacrifice, by means of the particular actions found in the Last Supper itself.

But as a matter of fact, it is not necessary to resort to this particular solution as the only way in which the development of the Eucharist can be described. To some extent, the theological point of view maintained in the preceding paragraph is essential to our discussion. Yet, as the best modern scholarship is now making obvious, it is simply not true that the Christian Eucharist is a perversion of the historic intention of the historic Jesus on the historic occasion of the Last Supper. The opening-up of the field of rabbinical studies, combined with a more careful analysis of Jewish customs and ceremonies during the latter part of the first century B.C. and during the early Christian era, has provided a considerable Jewish background for Christian sacramentalism and has given the *coup de grâce* to the older 'liberal Protestant' dismissal of sacramental and sacrificial worship as alien to the whole Christian 'idea.' More particularly, discoveries in this field have indicated, plainly and unequivocally, that the New Testament material concerning the Eucharist, both in its origins and in its development, is accurate enough so far is it goes (with whatever variations and modifications particular writers or particular circumstances may have introduced); on the other hand the alleged paucity of material is to be explained by the fact that it was hardly necessary to give long and detailed accounts of what was simply taken for granted both by the writer and by those for whom he wrote.

It is not our purpose to cover this vast field. It has already been explored in scholarly fashion by many writers, most notably in recent years by two Anglicans who have given us the results of their careful and thorough investigations: Dr. Felix L. Cirlot in his invaluable study *The Early Eucharist*, which not only surveys the entire subject and covers the earlier work that has been done by scholars, but also breaks new ground and provides highly important conclusions; and Dom Gregory Dix, whose great book *The Shape of the Liturgy* is an exhaustive study of the subject of eucharistic origins, and is rendered all the more valuable because it carries this investigation down through the later centuries in terms of the actual liturgical forms that were used to celebrate the Lord's Supper. A smaller book, also in English, should be mentioned among the many in English, German, and French that are available; this is Dr. Frank Gavin's *Jewish Antecedents of the Christian Sacraments*, a convenient and by no means outdated preliminary survey of the subject.

In our own study, however, we are assuming the validity of the conclusions reached in the massive works mentioned above. Our purpose is to discuss the Christian

Sacrifice in its wide range, against the background of the Christian dogmatic position and in the context of the faith that the Christian Church, in which and by which the Sacrifice is offered, is the Body of Christ. It will suffice in this chapter, therefore, if we sketch the New Testament origins of the Christian Eucharist as they may be reconstructed today, thanks to the efforts of the scholars whose writings may always be used as a reference for and a check upon our own description. Our concern will be specifically theological; what was the *meaning*, the underlying *intention*, of the action at the Last Supper and in the primitive Christian community? Could it develop, logically and rightly, into the full meaning and intention that the Body of Christ has maintained as the heart of its characteristic expression in worship?

But first we must say something of what *happened*, so far as this can be done. The first point to be made is that Judaism, in the time of our Lord, was by no means the purely ethico-religious system that has often been portrayed for us. Synagogue-worship was a simple affair, and the majority of the residents in the Holy Land, as also in the *diaspora*, had to be content with such worship for most of their public gatherings. Yet the Temple in Jerusalem remained the center of the worship of the Jewish people; the traditional rites, sacrificial in nature, were carried out there; the Jew regarded it as a high privilege, indeed a necessity, to make a pilgrimage to the Temple and take part in its worship, if it were at all possible for him to do so.

Even more significant, however, is the custom of Jewish family meals and family rites, which were definitely of a religious nature. The Passover Meal has long been familiar to us; in recent years we have learned of the Kiddush, a meal held before great feasts or the Sabbath, presided over by the father of the family or the rabbi with his company of disciples. Even more recently it has been discovered that small bands of religiously minded men, forming a family-in-faith, would frequently meet together for a meal, during which there would be long spiritual discussion and religious actions of blessings and praise. Some reflection of this sort of meal is probably furnished by the stories of the miraculous feedings, found in all our gospels, as well as in the reference in the Lucan (24:13-35) Emmaus tale to the way in which Jesus was known 'in the breaking of bread.' He had often presided, it would seem, at just such a religio-social meal; his way of doing this, his actions, and his words were so distinctive that they could be remembered as being uniquely and peculiarly his.

Incidentally, although it does not bear on our present study, Jewish sacramentalism—in its own terms, and with that almost complete merging of material and spiritual which was natural to the religiously monistic mind of the Jew in worship (a point well handled by Dr. Gavin in the book to which we have referred)—is also expressed in the baptism for proselytes, which at the time of Jesus was a fairly normal and regular practice. Of this, the baptism of John the Baptizer was a variant, the difference being that he was so convinced of the defection of the Jewish people from the will of God that he was prepared to insist that they *all* needed believer's baptism.

It may be concluded, from what we now have

learned of the customs of the Jewish rabbi and his disciples, as well as the family ritual of the typical Jewish home, that Jesus was in the habit of holding frequent meals of this type. In this sense, the Last Supper is only one—but the concluding one—of a series. Yet this is not the whole story, because the tradition implies that certain specific actions, normal in the rite, were accompanied by certain specific words, not normal therein, on the occasion of this concluding supper at which Jesus and his 'little flock' were gathered. The meaning of those actions in relation to those particular words is important for our purpose in determining what precisely was the intention in the mind of the historic Jesus, as he met for the last time with his disciples in the common meal. Was this sufficiently like the meaning that the later Christian community found in its central rite to warrant our saying that there is no contradiction between the 'mind' of Jesus and the 'mind' of the Church?

As to the meal itself, the Last Supper with its peculiarly religious setting, there is little difficulty. The New Testament accounts are found in Matthew 26:26-30; Mark 14:22-6; Luke 22:14-20; First Corinthians 11:23-6. The disciples gathered with our Lord, in the Upper Room, for their common meal, with its accompaniment of spiritual fellowship and discussion. The meal was opened, as was customary, with the usual ceremonies, including the breaking of bread by the master of the table, and a common participation in the broken bread by all present. Then followed the repast, with conversation on religious matters—it is not unlikely that the so-called 'table talk' of Jesus, reported in the thirteenth and fourteenth chapters of the Fourth Gospel, is the kind of discussion (although of course not a precise report of the discussion at the Last Supper itself) that must have taken place. At the conclusion of the meal, once again there was a common participation in a customary action. A cup of wine, mixed with water, was blessed by the master of the table, and all those present shared in this. The meal was then concluded; and the events thereafter, following the singing of the usual psalm of thanksgiving, are given us in the gospels. Jesus went into the garden of Gethsemane, where he was arrested, and was then imprisoned. The trial followed, later in the night and in the morning, and Jesus was taken away to be crucified.

So far as the meal is concerned, the various incidents seem to be those natural to a Jewish family or rabbinical gathering. As the dating in the Fourth Gospel would appear to make plain, this was not the Passover feast; The Church historically has followed the Johannine chronology, and rightly. The Passover reference, as we shall see, is both appropriate and inevitable, and springs either from Pauline sources or from such sources as St. Paul later found at hand; this was thrown back to modify the chronology that the synoptic gospels present. Neither does this meal appear to have been the traditional Kiddush before a feast, as modern scholars have pointed out. The best interpretation is that it was the usual meal, and therefore not in externals unlike many of those the disciples were accustomed to enjoy with their Master during the days they were associated with him in his work.

What gave the unique and special quality to this meal was not that it was the last supper that the disciples

were to have with their Master, but the way in which he
interpreted his actions at the supper. For it is part of the
continuing and undisputed early Christian tradition that
when Jesus blessed and broke the bread, distributing to
those who were of the table fellowship, he used words that
associated the broken bread with his own body, saying
'This my body broken for you.' In the thanksgiving over
the cup of blessing, at the close of the meal, he also used
special words, which were probably these: 'This the new
covenant ratified in my blood.' If the words we have just
given, used over the bread and wine, are not the exact
words our Lord spoke, they are close enough to them to
indicate what the meal was taken to suggest. What was this?

The meal the disciples had with their Master meant
that the death Jesus knew was in store for him in the immediate future was to be the means whereby a new relationship would be set up between God and men. By sharing
in the broken bread and the cup of blessing, the disciples
were proleptically participating in the benefits that would
come to them and to Israel through that death. The bread
was broken, as his body was to be broken; the wine was
shared, as a participation in the new covenant that would
be brought into being through his sacrifice for his people.
By this action, even before the death itself occurred, Jesus
set the stamp of sacrificial offering upon his coming death
and made it possible for the members of his 'little flock' to
share already in that which the death was to accomplish,
and which, as the event proved, they were to be instrumental in making available for others as they went out

presently to proclaim the crucified Lord who had 'brought life and immortality to light through the gospel.'

We are not to be unmindful of the time element, however; this means that we are not to read into the actual thinking of the Master or of his disciples more than is actually there. [The fullness of meaning is to be found in the way the disciples and the early Christian community discovered that the continued meal, now carried on (once Jesus was crucified) in 'his remembrance,' made his presence an effective and effectual reality.]It may not be certain, as some scholars affirm, that our Lord *directly ordered* this 'memorial'; in any event, the meal would have been continued by the 'little flock' as their regular table fellowship. The probability is that Jesus did say, or at least imply, that the group was to continue as a group after his death, until the coming of the Kingdom—with which his death was inextricably associated, as the necessary precondition for God to give that kingdom to men. If they were to continue, they would continue as the fellowship of followers of the Nazarene; in fact, they were later called 'those of the Nazarene way.' If this were so, they would indubitably persist in the fellowship at table. Hence, the intention if not the explicit direction of Jesus was that the table fellowship, with the breaking of bread and the sharing of the cup of blessing, should be 'his memorial'—that is to say, should have the meaning and the effect of bringing the benefits of his death into the midst of the continuing fellowship. The repetition of the meal, which would have occurred in any case, with the particular actions performed in the fashion in which he indicated, would be like the

ancient Passover feast. In the Passover the benefits brought
to the Jewish people at the deliverance from the Egyptians
were made a present and effective reality as they repeated
the action supposed to have been associated with that deliverance, as they believed it had actually occurred in the
historical events recorded in their Scriptures. So the repetition of the meal, with Jesus 'in remembrance,' according to
the pattern he had established with his disciples, would
bring the benefits of his sacrifice for the Jewish people into
the immediate present, until such time as the Kingdom of
God should be established and the new covenant come as a
patent reality.

The Last Supper, then, did three things that otherwise would have been left undone. It set the mark of sacrifice upon the events that were to transpire the next day:
Jesus gave his life as a free offering, that through his death
God's Kingdom might be brought in, or at least its coming
might be made a certainty. This is the first fact of importance to be attached to the Supper. The second is that by
this Supper, with the particular actions and words accom-
panying it, Jesus made certain that the circle of his followers, associated with him through his ministry up to that
time, should also be associated with him, by foretaste, in
the sacrifice he was to make. By that association, which
would include not only his death but whatever was involved in that death, they would be participants in the new
covenant that was to be established finally and openly when
God gave his Kingdom. Thirdly in doing this, he also
brought about the creation of a body or community or fellowship which, under the new covenant, would find its

natural and inevitable center in the common meal, and which would also be the 'first fruits' of that fulfilled new covenant that it was his task to create between God and man.

There is no reason whatsoever, apart from purely *a priori* assumptions, to deny to the human mind of the historic Jesus each and all of these intentions. The later development of eucharistic thought as found in St. Paul and in St. John is then in no sense a contradiction of the 'mind' of Jesus, but an amplification of a purpose that was not only latent in all his words and actions but to some degree explicitly stated by our Lord himself. To this we shall turn in a few pages. At the moment there is one other point to be made.

The human mind of Jesus was necessarily limited by the particular circumstances and situation in which he lived as incarnate. It is part of the orthodox dogma of the Incarnation that the eternal reality of the Word of God was united, intimately and directly—to use the traditional formula, hypostatically or personally—with complete and full and genuine human nature. Such human nature must necessarily include a human mind. And a truly human mind involves those 'conditionings' (as the phrase has it) which belong to a man living in a given time and place, with a given historical background and outlook. Now it is precisely in the historic milieu of Judaism, with its particular religious orientation, that Jesus lived. His human mind was a Jewish mind of his own time and place. It was under those conditions and in that fashion that the Divine Word acted and spoke. We are then justified in saying that the full intention of God in the actions that the historic Jesus performed in the Last Supper included more than the human mind of Jesus himself may have foreseen. The Last Supper was not only what we have described. It was also the essential historic action or set of actions needed by God, on the human level, so that he might establish for his children a sacrificial rite by which they might enter into the full significance of the self-offering of incarnate God. It was a way in which they might be knit together in a religious fellowship united with that incarnate God. It was the rite whereby they might be given the 'bread which came down from heaven' and the 'wine which would make glad their hearts,' that through this bread and wine they might feed on the crucified and triumphantly risen humanity of incarnate God. This larger purpose in the divine intention the historic human events could not in and of themselves express, without moving out of their place in history. It is this that was the inevitable and purposed consequence of those actions that incarnate God himself, in the terms and under the conditions of his incarnate life, performed.

The task of St. Paul and St. John was to bring into clearer light the divine intention that was operative in the Last Supper, as well as to work out, on the human level, the implications of that intention which (as we have seen) may properly be regarded as already present in the Upper Room itself.

The Pauline position, incidentally expounded by the apostle in First Corinthians 10:16-21 and 11:20-34, is in essentials perfectly definite and clear, whatever may be the uncertainties about particular details. The central action of Christian worship is directly related to that which the apostle received 'of the Lord.' It is an unnecessary hypothesis to say that this was some direct revelation of the risen Christ to St. Paul; on the contrary, we may assume that it was given him 'from the Lord,' through the community of believers in which he found the Christian gospel proclaimed and the Christian life a reality. That which the Lord Jesus did in the Upper Room was to be carried on by the Christian Church, with the plain explanation that 'as often as ye eat this bread and drink this cup, ye do shew the Lord's death, till he come.'

With this Pauline passage should be associated his extended reference, also found in the First Corinthians (5:7-8), to the fact declared in Christian faith and experience: 'Christ our Passover is sacrificed for us.' Here we have stated the relation of both the Last Supper and the Christian 'breaking of bread' to the Jewish Passover. It is a relation that probably derives from St. Paul himself or from circles with which the apostle was familiar. This conception is responsible for the Markan impression that the Supper was intended by Jesus to be a Christian substitute for the Passover since its institution is portrayed as taking place at the Passover Meal. The reference in Luke (22:15) to the 'desire with which [Jesus] desired to eat this Passover' seems to deny the Markan idea. Luke suggests that the expressed wish of Jesus was not to be fulfilled until the coming of the Kingdom of God.

In any event, the Pauline reference to the Passover, with its intimation of forgiveness and a new covenant be-

tween God and his people, like that established by God
with the Jewish people in the older dispensation, is a correct reading of the *ultimate* meaning of the Eucharist. Furthermore, the other Pauline declaration, in First Corinthians (10:16-21), that the tables of demons and the table of
the Lord were so antithetical that it was wickedness to
partake of the former when one was a partaker of the latter,
since the communion at the Lord's table is in the body and
blood of Christ—'the cup of blessing which we bless, is it
not the communion of the blood of Christ; the bread which
we break, is it not the communion of the body of Christ?'—
makes it apparent that for St. Paul, as later for St. John, the
'Spirit-infused food' (as Loofs has called it) that was received in the Christian sacrament was no mere external
symbol of Christ's life, but was indeed the very participation in that life conceived as somehow genuinely present
in the 'body of Christ' and the 'blood of Christ.'

The emphasis in St. Paul is on the *sacrificial* nature
of the rite, however—at least, in that the 'shewing-forth' of
the Lord's death was a memorial in the Jewish sense, rather
than in our much modified modern sense. To 'shew forth
the Lord's death' meant to plead and to placard before God
and men that which had been accomplished on Calvary, a
pleading and a placarding made possible for those who were
'partakers of the Lord's table' because they were those who
made their communion in the body and blood of Christ.
Here is the central significance of the rite for the Pauline
theology. It is the effectual statement of and the active
entrance upon that which the Lord once for all accomplished by his passion and death. But for St. Paul, as for the

later Christian Church, the passion and death of Christ cannot be separated from his other 'mighty acts.' The implied teaching of the apostle could not be better summed up than in the words of the American Prayer Book eucharistic canon: 'we, thy humble servants, do celebrate and make here, before thy divine majesty, with these thy holy gifts, which we now offer unto thee, the memorial thy Son hath commanded us to make, having in remembrance his blessed passion and precious death, his mighty resurrection and glorious ascension, rendering unto thee most hearty thanks for the innumerable benefits procured unto us by the same.'

The element in the Christian sacrifice suggested by the words 'most hearty thanks' is essential to the entire rite, both in its dominical origin and in its Pauline setting. It is an established fact that all Jewish blessings were in the form of thanksgivings; and it is known that the atmosphere of a *chaburah* meal, as well as of all Jewish table ritual, was one of praise to God for his mighty acts on man's behalf, for the covenant between God and man, for his gifts to his children, and for his continued blessings upon them. The formulae Jesus would have used at the Last Supper, as at the other table meals with his 'little flock,' were words of praise to God, beginning with 'Blessed be thou [*or* Thanks be to thee] for . . .' The gifts of bread and wine would have been named after the initial thanksgiving and praise. This would also have been the atmosphere and setting with which St. Paul was familiar.

Yet the thanksgiving, so far as the Last Supper was concerned, would have included as an undertone the fact, obvious in Christ's own mind and made clear by his actions to the disciples who were present, that the death of our Lord was imminent; hence it would have been thanksgiving for the coming sacrifice. And for the primitive community, not least for St. Paul himself, it is psychologically absurd to suggest that the typical Jewish thanksgiving ritual could have been followed without constant reference to that awful fact which was indeed the chief occasion for any Christian thanks and praise offered to God—the death of Christ, whereby men had been given the entrance into the Kingdom of God, now and to come. The death of Christ was not isolated from his triumph, of course; but, on the other hand, it is a very naïve reconstruction of the rite which would assert that the death was overlooked and forgotten in the joy of the resurrection. 'Death is swallowed up in victory,' but the fact of death, and above all the fact that he who brought the victory was that same One who had died, could never be forgotten, neglected, minimized, or overlooked.

So one can readily see that the Christian 'breaking of bread,' as reflected in the Pauline testimony, was a thanksgiving rite in which the sacrifice of Christ was pleaded before God, 'shewn forth' until the kingdom should come in its transcendent glory, while at the same time in this rite Christian believers fed upon the risen yet crucified life of the Lord who had brought them out of darkness into his glorious light.

It is at this point that the Johannine witness is important. For the feeding upon Christ that was central to the 'breaking of bread' was a feeding upon the life of One who was himself 'the bread from heaven.' The likelihood that the sixth chapter of the Fourth Gospel, from which these words are quoted, is a long meditation on the Eucharist, as understood in Ephesus at the turn of the first century, does not for a moment reduce its profound importance and value to us in understanding the meaning of the rite for both earlier and later generations of Christians. The relation of the Eucharist to the miracle of the feeding, which as we have seen is probably a recollection of the table fellowship of our Lord and his disciples, indicates that the whole intention of the passage is to make manifest that which is hidden in the great Christian sacrament. Jesus is represented as affirming that he is 'the bread of life,' who takes the place of the manna given to the fathers of Israel. So the eucharistic food, which is described as 'the flesh of the Son of Man' and 'his blood,' is the life of the Christian believer who has benefited by the new Passover which Jesus himself both effected and in his inner reality truly was. Here is real and abiding life, for 'my flesh is meat indeed, and my blood is drink indeed,' and 'he that eateth of this bread shall live for ever.'

On the other hand, it is made plain that while the actual eating and drinking are physical facts—for the evangelist uses the Greek verbs normally employed for the actual eating and drinking—the bread that is received and the wine that is drunk are not to be understood in a purely material way. 'Spirit' and 'life' are not to be contained wholly within, although they are conveyed through, physical bread and wine. Here in a primitive form is the distinction that led the later theologians of the Church to distinguish between the material sign and the thing signified, or, in medieval thought between the accidents and the substance of the sacrament. But this distinction is suggested without in any way reducing the eucharistic body and blood to mere empty tokens; tokens they are, but tokens that partake in that which they signify and by so doing give 'life unto the world.'

The Epistle to the Hebrews, with its constant development of the fashion in which Christ is the substance of which the old Jewish priesthood, sacrifice, and worship are the shadow and image, has its place in giving us a rounded understanding of the New Testament view of the Eucharist. It is only a prejudiced critic who can rule out of this document all trace of sacerdotal and sacrificial worship; the fact is that the worship which is hinted by the tractate is the fulfilment in Christ himself of all that has gone before in Judaism. He it is who as High Priest has entered into the 'temple not made with hands'; and who, himself being the 'living way' to the Father, has made it possible for men to have free access to 'the throne of grace.' It is his blood that was offered to take away sin, as 'the blood of bulls and of goats' could never do; and it is in him and by him, as 'the pioneer of our salvation' and as the 'author and perfecter of our faith,' that it is possible for men to approach 'boldly' their Father in heaven.

This sacrificial and sacerdotal setting is natural if Christianity is seen as a religion concerned, even in its primitive days, with a sacrificial rite that supplanted and rendered unnecessary the ancient Jewish ceremonies. In the well-known words of St. Thomas Aquinas, we are able to affirm,

Types and shadows have their ending,
For the newer rite is here.

The 'newer rite' is that action which the early Christians believed that their risen Lord had commanded while on earth,
when 'in the night in which he was betrayed, he took
bread . . .' The connection of this action with the theology
presented in Hebrews is obvious to anyone who does not
begin with a prejudice against it. One might almost say
that if there had not been clear proof that such an action
did exist, it would be necessary to argue logically to its
existence. Otherwise, the faith of the author of the sermon
or tractate which we call Hebrews would have been hang-
ing in mid-air, with nothing to root it to the historical
facts with which it was concerned, or relate it to the eternal
reality those facts were believed to have declared.

The earliest Christian community, then, as represented to us in the New Testament, had as its chief action
of worship the 'breaking of bread' or 'giving of thanks,' by
which was meant the eucharistic rite. This common Christian action, together with 'the apostles' doctrine and fellowship,' distinguished the Christian community from all
others. The Acts of the Apostles, whether dated in the third
quarter of the first century or considered with some few
critics, as an anti-Marcionite document of the second century, gives in its second chapter probably an accurate enough
picture of the nature of the Christian 'way' and its peculiar-
ities. There, in addition to the eucharistic action and the
acceptance of the apostolic gospel and fellowship, we find
a sharing of support in a community of goods, participation

(so far as Jerusalem Christians were concerned) in the Temple worship natural to Jews, a common sharing in prayer, and a common interest in the conversion of others to the new gospel. The spiritual quality of the community's life is also portrayed for us, in the striking words, 'gladness and singleness of heart,' as applied probably to the Christians at their meals of fellowship.

The double reference to 'breaking of bread' in this section of Acts, coupled with St. Paul's reprimand addressed to the Corinthians in his First Epistle to those enthusiastic but somewhat misguided believers, makes it apparent that while the primitive community had at first followed the pattern of the Jewish table meal, with its combination of a religious action and a social repast, it presently became necessary to separate the two. The Jewish custom was to begin and end the table fellowship with special religious exercises, prayer and thanksgiving first over bread and last over wine, and to have the supper between these two. Doubtless, at the beginning, the supper itself had been orderly enough, with high religious discourse; this surely was true among the Jews and had unquestionably been the fact at the Last Supper itself. This, too, is evidently the picture that is given us in the second chapter of Acts. But as Christianity spread into the Gentile world, among those whose background was not the generally sober one of Judaism in its religious practice, it was inevitable that abuses should appear. The situation in Corinth, which St. Paul was concerned to correct, was doubtless not the only occasion upon which unseemly conduct had occurred at Christian religious gatherings. The solution of the problem was simple though not easy. It was to separate the memorial of the death of Christ, the 'shewing-forth,' from the fellowship meal and conviviality.

This separation, reflected perhaps in First Corinthians and certainly found in later times, meant that the first and the last actions at the Jewish meal, as it had been taken over by the Christian community, were combined in a single rite. The middle part of the Jewish table fellowship, which had been the common supper, was made into another gathering. Hence there were two associations of Christians, one to hold the memorial of the sacrifice of the death of Christ, as the characteristic religious action of those who were members of his Body; the other to enjoy a fellowship of believers, or (in later language) to hold the *agapè*. Perhaps it is as well here as at some other point to stress this distinction between the *anamnesis*, which is translated 'memorial' or 'remembrance' in most of our literature on the subject, and the *agapè*. But the distinction must not be stressed to a point where it is implied that originally the two had not been very intimately related.

It is probable that when the separation of the two elements in the Jewish table fellowship was necessarily made by the Christians, the peculiarly 'anamnetic' nature of the memorial of Christ's redemptive action was more strongly emphasized. Up to that time, there had doubtless been a certain tendency to balance the elements in the Christian religio-social gathering, the memorial of our Lord's passion being set against the highly joyous community fellowship that would have marked the common supper. Even if the note had been one of 'solemn joy,' there would have been no sharp pointing-up of the memorial itself as *the sole object* of the entire ceremonial meal. But with the removal of the *agapè* from the memorial, it is natural that the latter would be given a distinctive importance, a vivid reality, which belonged to itself alone.

In no sense, however, was this a *new* significance; it was, on the contrary, a sharpening and heightening of an already present significance. It may be conjectured that it is precisely this sharpening and heightening that led to the specific association of the Christian *anamnesis* with the Passover, as found in First Corinthians. If the 'shewing-forth of the Lord's death,' with participation in his continuing life through 'the communion of the body of Christ' and 'the communion of the blood of Christ,' was the sole significance of the now isolated Christian action in worship, then the analogy with the Jewish Passover was plain enough. The theological development, by virtue of which Christ's death was construed as 'a ransom for many,' while his Resurrection was taken to be—in a phrase entirely true to the New Testament witness—'the opening of the kingdom of heaven to all believers,' would parallel and implement the liturgical development. The evidence in the Matthean account of the Last Supper, in which 'the remission of sins' is explicitly mentioned as part of the significance of the events of the Last Supper and Calvary, is sufficiently convincing at this point when we remember that the Matthean gospel was probably written at the close of the first century, and that its language is often a reflection of a settled and sometimes liturgical use of words—as is shown in the formalized

Our Father and the balanced style of the Beatitudes in their Matthean form.

The final point to which attention must be directed is the way in which both St. Paul and St. John envisage the relation of a Christian believer to the Lord and to other believers. For St. Paul the Christian is member of 'a body.' This does not imply simply that all Christians are 'members one of another,' although that is of course true, but that Christians are members of the Body of Christ, whose life enters into them and works through them. St. John, using the metaphor of the vine and the branches, in which it is suggested that the believer is like the branch that would perish if the healthy life of the vine did not flow through it, makes plain to us the intimate relationship that he felt existed between Christ the Word and those who were believers in him. For both of these writers, to be a Christian meant nothing else than to share in 'the en-Christed life.' This in turn meant nothing else than to be a member of the Christian fellowship; and the Christian fellowship was no accidental affair but the very Body of Christ himself. The Johannine emphasis upon living in Christ as Christ lives in the believer is simply a variant of this theme, in that writer's own idiom. Still another variant can be found in First Peter, with its simple and explicit assertion that 'ye are a royal priesthood, an holy nation, a peculiar people.' For this means that the old Israel, chosen by God and built upon God's will, has been supplanted by the new Israel. The existence of the new is continuous with the old, but it is built upon the Messiah who has reconstituted it as a new people. From Christ is derived its peculiar life, its priestly

function, and its unique vocation to bring salvation to men.
The relation of all this to the Christian Sacrifice is
obvious. The characteristic and life-giving action of the
Body of Christ, the True Vine and its branches, the royal
priesthood and holy nation, is the celebration and commemoration—that is, the *anamnesis*—of the redemptive
action of God in Christ. From the Upper Room down to
the day of the latest New Testament writer this was the
normal and distinctive way in which Christians behaved
when they did not forsake 'the assembling' of themselves
together to 'offer the sacrifice of praise to God continually.'
Or, in our own idiom, the Eucharist is the way in which
the Christian Church which is the mystical Body of Christ,
naturally and rightly worships God, offering the 'sacrifice
of praise and thanksgiving' as it celebrates and makes 'the
memorial [his] Son hath commanded us to make.'

3] *The Eucharist in the Early Church*

The history of the hundred and more years after the New Testament period is, so far as Christian worship is concerned, the history of the continuing explication of elements already found in New Testament literature. Language may have changed, but the main lines of development were laid down in the days of the primitive community, and the differences to be observed in later periods are not those that come from a departure from the early witness, but those that involve a deeper penetration into the significance of that witness.

Even if it be true, as we may well be inclined to think, that the influence upon Christian worship of the so-called mystery religions has in recent years been underestimated, in reaction from the tendency in the past to overestimate it, the fact remains that the contribution which the nomenclature and the forms of these various cults made to Christian worship was by way of drawing out ideas and practices that were not in themselves alien to the primitive Christian notion of worship emerging from the Jewish pattern. To the Jewish background attention was given in the last chapter. The elaboration of forms of worship was inevitable as the Christian community, whether under outside influence or not, came to realize the true significance of the action in which it was engaged. The formalized language,

supplanting the free liturgy of earlier days, was natural
when the Church became settled and was obliged to provide for all sorts and conditions of men in a way that would
not expose them to the vagaries of individual leaders. The
sacrificial references and the descriptions applied to the
eucharistic elements, while influenced once again by the
new environment into which Christianity was brought,
were directly in line with the teaching about the *anamnesis*
and the body and blood of Christ that is to be found in St.
Paul's incidental remarks on the primitive Eucharist.

Our task in this chapter is not to discuss the way in
which the several extant documents illustrate liturgical development, although this is a fascinating study and could
well engage our attention. Neither is it to show that there
is a marked similarity in all the accounts of the early
Church's worship. Our object is to give some insight into
the development of the eucharistic *idea*. This is reflected in
the liturgical documents, but it is shown as well in incidental references in some of the apologists and other early
writers. The *idea*, as we intend it, is the notion of the meaning of the Eucharist, its centrality and importance: here we
shall be preparing for our later chapters, in which the several aspects of the Christian Sacrifice will be noticed and
their interrelationship studied, with constant reference to
the all-controlling factor which is the Church as the mystical Body of Christ.

The very term 'sacrifice' suggests a starting place
for our inquiry. For it is often and inaccurately contended
that the notion of sacrifice as applied to the Eucharist has
no real place in the early period of Christianity. Now it is

certainly true that it is not until St. Cyprian (in his 63rd Epistle) that we discover the explicit association of the offering of the Eucharist with 'the passion of Christ,' undertaken by the Church's minister as the Church's sacrifice. But the note struck in St. Cyprian is not absent in earlier writings. One of the most interesting documents of the first two hundred years of the Church's life is the *Didache*, which is now usually dated in the first quarter of the second century. We discover in Chapter 16 of the document a clear reference to the Eucharist as an offering; the explicit association with the passion of our Lord is not to be found, but the sacrificial element is by no means lacking. Nor does the *Didache* stand alone in this respect. In the epistles of St. Ignatius of Antioch, the eucharistic action is frequently mentioned; these letters, written at the close of the first century, are addressed to the various churches known to the writer, and deal with important matters of Christian order and faith. Not only does St. Ignatius speak of the Eucharist as 'the medicine of immortality,' a phrase that bears resemblance to the language of the mystery cults and implies the highest conception of the significance of the eucharistic elements; he also refers to the action itself in language that leaves no doubt that he regarded it as 'the flesh of our Saviour Christ' celebrated in 'the place of sacrifice' (cf. his letters to the Smyrneans, 6, and to the Ephesians, 5 and 20).

The writings of Justin Martyr, especially his famous *Apologies*, are another case in point. The description of the Eucharist (*Apology* 1, 65-7), whether it be that concerned with an ordinary observance of the Lord's Day, or the special Easter celebration to which he devotes particular attention, makes clear that for him the central action of the Christian Church is the sacramental offering. In this the Last Supper is 're-called' and the communicants both offer the fruits of the earth which become the means of Christ's presence, and by reception share in Christ's 'flesh and blood.' The very actions he cites as part of the rite are so related to the New Testament evidence as to make it plain that the whole intention is that which St. Paul himself indicates in First Corinthians. Furthermore, in his *Dialogue with Trypho*, Justin explicitly calls the Eucharist a sacrifice (*c.*117).

Clement of Alexandria, whose thinking was Neoplatonic in mold, is none the less explicit enough about the Eucharist as 'hallowed food,' and its significance as conveying the risen life of Jesus Christ—who for him is always the Logos made flesh that he might bring to men the knowledge of God. In St. Irenaeus's polemic against gnosticism, the *Adversus Haereses*, the Eucharist is referred to as the body and blood of Christ, the offering of it as 'a pure sacrifice to God'; the entire rite is mentioned in contexts that relate it to the Incarnation itself and also to the deed of God in the Incarnate Word for the redemption of the world. (IV, 18. 4-6).

These are a few of the early writers who may be cited, among many others, as illustrating the eucharistic *idea*. The final and conclusive writer, since from him spring the liturgies of both East and West, is Hippolytus of Rome, whose *Apostolic Tradition* has particular importance in liturgical study, but whose value for us is that he sums up the idea of the Eucharist as being a true 'oblation of the Holy Church' associated with the offering by the people of their gifts but not exhausted in that offering, since it is related directly to the redemptive offering of Christ. Furthermore, Hippolytus is important in that, despite his use of what has often been called 'symbolic' language, he leaves no doubt at all that when he speaks of the 'antitype' of Christ's body as the bread in the Eucharist, he means not a bare symbolism but a vital association of the bread with the body of Christ. Thus he almost foreshadows the realism of later writers like St. Ambrose.

Detailed quotations and discussion of the material in these and other early Christian documents may be found in such a book as Dom Gregory Dix's *The Shape of the Liturgy*. Our purpose here has not been to give an exhaustive account of the material; in fact, we have barely touched the surface and have left unmentioned much that is of value while raising problems that require trained Patristic scholarship to handle adequately. But we have mentioned a few names to indicate that the whole trend of development in the early days of the Church's life is not away from the kind of position that is found in the New Testament, but rather is in the direction of amplifying and more deeply penetrating that position. If, with the writers already cited, we recall later ones such as St. Cyprian, to whom reference has been made; St. Cyril of Jerusalem in his *Catechetical Lectures;* the Antiochene school (with particular attention to Theodore of Mopsuestia, who had much to say in his *Catechetical Lectures* on the Eucharist); and western Christians such as St. Augustine, especially in his sermons, and before him St. Ambrose in his *De Sacramentis* and his tract on 'the Mysteries,' we shall find that there is an astonishing consensus in regard to what we have called the eucharistic *idea*. To that idea, in its widest sense, we must now turn.

For all these men, the Eucharist is first of all central in the entire Christian scheme of things. Not one of the writers we have mentioned, or any other of whom we are aware, has any doubt whatsoever about this point. Christian worship is always and pre-eminently eucharistic. The way in which it is mentioned is in itself an indication that it is even 'taken for granted.' The facility with which it is used as a proof in connection with discussion of major Christian doctrines shows that it could be assumed to be the common action of all Christian believers. To worship meant for the Christians, in a phrase from an earlier writer, 'to make Eucharist.' Temple worship was no longer possible for Christians when they were not in the Holy Land and in Jerusalem; after the fall of that city and the destruction of the Temple, it would have been out of the question in any case. The Gentile converts did not have the Jewish loyalty to the Temple; it was not part of their religious heritage. Nor was worship in the synagogue, which was doubtless frequented during the earliest days of the Christian community. Apart from such private gatherings as might have occurred in homes, or such associations of friends as might have met for what we should today call 'prayer meetings,' there was no worship in the Christian Church except the offering of the Eucharist.

And the Eucharist was consistently understood to

be the Christian equivalent of or parallel to the Jewish sacrifices that it replaced, as its Lord himself had been the
substance of that which the Jewish sacrifices prefigured. As
early as the Epistle to the Hebrews this was plainly implied;
the terminology later employed in the Church leaves no
doubt that Christians did not feel that they lacked a sacrificial service. The Eucharist was an offering in which gifts
were brought to God, blessed by him, and then distributed
to the needy. But it was more than that; it was an offering
in which the Church thanked God for the redemption
wrought by Christ, pleaded the Cross before the Father, and
believed itself to be associated in that oblation. We cannot
stress too much the sense in which the term *anamnesis* was
used at this time; unquestionably, it meant recalling into the
present the crucial event that had occurred in the past. This
was the pleading of Christ's sacrifice, and in this pleading
the sacrifice was offered to God. There is not the slightest
evidence that the early Church thought it was 'sacrificing
Christ afresh' or repeating in any bloody sense the death on
Calvary. Rather, it was an entrance into and a pleading of
what the Anglican Prayer Book calls 'that one oblation of
himself, once offered.' The early Church thought it was
offering a sacrifice—a sacrifice that was not 'bloody' but
that was commemorative in the profound meaning given
to *anamnesis*.

　　　It is impossible to understand what was meant by
this unless we realize that for the early Church the consciousness of a unity in Christ by common participation in
his Body was the center of life. It has already been noticed
that this was the New Testament assumption and teaching.

It is equally significant that for the early Church the sense of membership in the crucified and risen Lord was at the heart of life and experience. But if the Church was the Body of Christ, then the self-sacrifice of Christ on Calvary was indeed the sacrifice of the Church itself, since his Body was indubitably one with him. Therefore the event that had occurred historically in Palestine was not an event that was 'far away and long ago'; it was an event that was present in the Body of Christ. And when that Body, obeying Christ's precept and acting according to his example, offered the Eucharist, it was making visible and tangible before men, and placarding and pleading before God, the historic and actual offering on Calvary, to which at the Last Supper Christ had given this particular significance and intention.

This is why it is possible for St. Augustine to refer in his sermons, and elsewhere in his writings, to the identity of the eucharistic offering at the altar and the sacrifice of the Church as a whole to God in union with Christ. The reason we today find it difficult to grasp this idea is simply that we are not normally so keenly aware of our membership in the Body of Christ as the dominant and dominating factor in our spiritual lives. But for early Christians, this was so central and important that they could easily enter into the truth St. Augustine stated. The teaching about the sacrificial nature of the Eucharist, not only by the Bishop of Hippo but by all the early writers, is to be understood against this kind of background.

But if the Eucharist was central and was sacrificial in nature, within the context of the *anamnesis* and in the Body of Christ, it was also a genuine communion in the body and blood of Christ himself. Whether the mode of expression of this truth was the philosophical one of 'symbolism,' as it has been called, or the plain experiential one of realism (as in St. Ambrose, for example), the meaning is the same. For it cannot too often be recalled that the kind of symbolic language that prevailed in the philosophical and theological writings of that day was not the 'remote' symbolism of a later time but rather the Neoplatonic symbolism in which the sign partook of the nature of the thing signified. When St. Augustine refers to sacraments as *signa sacra*, and even when he uses the term *signaculum* (which probably could be best translated as 'tag'), he does not mean to suggest that the only connection between the *sign* and the *thing signified* is that of a pointer toward a spiritual reality. He means to say that in and by and with the 'tag' or sign, the thing that is signified is effectually given. Indeed, one of the difficulties in St. Augustine's own thought was how to put as strongly as he wished the reality of the divine gift, thus effectually signified, while at the same time retaining certain other aspects of Neoplatonic thought not so congruous as this one with the Christian experience so dear to him, but yet so much a part of his mind and his habits of thinking that he could hardly escape them.

On the other hand, the realism found in St. Ambrose, who seems almost directly to identify bread and wine with the body and blood of Christ, and in some of the Syrian writers whose language suggests the same thought, is not to be understood in anything like the crude sense in which it has sometimes been interpreted. The realism is the realism of frank and genuine experience; and it is note-worthy that those who were most realistic in this apparently 'crude' sense were the matter-of-fact workaday Christians, bishops, and administrators, rather than the theological minds of the time. It is perhaps inevitable that the plain Christian will interpret his eucharistic experience in a direct fashion that may sometimes shock subtler minds. Stark ex-periential realism must always be qualified by a more phil-osophically careful statement; but on the other hand, the danger that is present today, but was not in the period with which we are concerned, is that in the business of refining the realism we shall also refine away the facts of experi-ence that the realism is stating.

The precise fashion in which the elements of bread and wine, used in the Eucharist, were regarded as identified by the eucharistic action with the body and blood of Christ varied from theologian to theologian. But that there *was* such an identification, and that it was an identification in no merely figurative sense, is clearly the fact. So it was pos-sible to have a great variety in the expression of the central reality, ranging all the way from the sense of sheer identity that called the elements, after consecration, 'the body and blood of Christ,' *tout court*, to the more sophisticated Hip-polytan phrases about the 'antitype.' The significant point for us is that there was never any doubt about the pres-ence of Christ there, not incidentally but vitally and essen-tially associated with the bread and wine. Hence they were to be accorded the highest reverence, as is indicated in Hippolytus' warning to the communicants who, according to the custom of the time, took away some of the eucha-

ristic food for communion at home. Tertullian, too, has a
reference to the reverent and careful retaining of the food
for consumption at home. Certainly the full reverence later
developed by Western usage was not to be found within
the eucharistic action itself or in the way the elements were
taken in small receptacles, to the homes of believers and
'reserved' for consumption day by day. In the Eastern communions even today this kind of reverence is not to be
found. But we know very well that what appears to us as
indifference does not bespeak a 'low' view of the nature
of the presence or of the intimate association of that presence with the elements themselves.

　　　Still another aspect of the eucharistic *idea* in the
early Church is to be seen in the way in which the significance of the *total* eucharistic action was emphasized, rather
than particular parts or divisions of that action. So far as we
can discover, there seems to have been no trace of the tendency to isolate a particular moment or place for consecration, as in the later Western Church with the so-called
'words of institution' or in the later Eastern Church with
the 'invocation of the Holy Spirit.' The total *action*, which
normally included the representation of our Lord's actions
and words, as these were found in the New Testament tradition, evidently was taken to be the 'consecratory formula.'
It is likely, however, that such technical language as this
would have had little meaning to the early Church. It was
not so much a *formula* that was in mind as it was the *action*
in which the Church, after Christ's command and following his own acts, offered to God the elements of bread
and wine, and in thus doing made its *anamnesis* or memorial

of him. It was believed that when this was done, the 'promise of Christ' was fulfilled. He was present in the action and there offered himself to the faithful for their food, while they themselves pleaded his redemption before the Father. Indeed, it appears that sometimes it was not even considered necessary to use the account of the dominical 'institution.' If the *Didache* is to be trusted as representing anything other than an unusual and perhaps isolated group of believers, this may have been a *lacuna* in one whole section of the Syrian Church. Normally, however, such was not the case; and it is noteworthy that, so far as our evidence goes, the model found in the *Didache* did not persist in later times.

Nor was the sacrificial aspect of the Eucharist separated from the communion of the faithful. Sacrifice seems to have been the primary, over-all interpretation and understanding of the action, but communion in the sacrificial action was normal and regular. The sacrifice was offered each Sunday, as part of the routine life of the Christian fellowship; all those who were in good standing as communicants were expected to receive the holy food on that day at that service. There seems to be no trace of noncommunicating attendance at the sacrifice—at any rate, no trace of it as an expected and accepted practice. It was for later generations, especially in medieval times, to make those moves that would lead eventually to noncommunicating attendance as a normal practice in the Western Church, with occasional communion only on the part of the faithful. Indeed it might be said that noncommunication, for any prolonged period, on the part of an individual in the early

Church would have indicated that the person in question was under ecclesiastical discipline, and hence was not one of the faithful. The meaning of excommunication was very clearly and precisely 'ex-communication'; it was regarded as a dire penalty inflicted on those who knew that the normal and right way for a Christian to express his appurtenance to the Body of Christ was by regular participation in the Church's eucharistic action Sunday by Sunday.

Finally, the pervading and commanding quality of the life of the Christian in the early Church—certainly up to the end of the persecutions and the conversion of Constantine—was a joyous realization of common fellowship in the society of believers which was the Body of Christ. Even when Christian profession seemed to be conventional, the sense of common fellowship was still not absent. This explains the serious view that was taken of apostasy, the concern for those who were suspected of having denied or destroyed the fellowship in faith and in worship. Because this was the case, the setting in which the Christian Eucharist was offered was one of *common* participation.

In the earlier days, the bishop, and later one of the appointed presbyters, would preside at the Lord's Table. Assisting would be the deacons, whose task in the Sacrifice was to act as the aides for the bishop, or presiding officer. When it was the bishop who celebrated, he was surrounded by the presbyters who were present, forming his *corona* behind the table itself. The faithful Christians were there in numbers, each group playing its proper part; for the several offices such as 'acolyte,' all now known as the 'minor orders,' spring from actual work done by members of the congregation in the early days of Christianity. Active sharing in the whole rite was a way in which one's membership in the Body of Christ was exhibited and expressed.

The clergy, in their role at the common worship of the Body, did not act in a vicarious fashion for the faithful. On the contrary, they acted on behalf of the congregation, representing the congregation in its corporate action, performing that action as the agents of the congregation, but, even more significantly, representing the total Body of Christ, of which the particular local group was a focus. In addition, the unity of the whole Church was expressed by the fact that the actions that were the essence of the sacrifice were actions in which all Christians everywhere participated, carried on by ministers who were delegated to represent all Christians everywhere. A symbol of this unity is found in the ancient Roman use. The present rite of the commixture, with the *pax* (when the celebrant breaks a fragment of the priest's host and drops it into the chalice) has its origin in the Church of Rome in early days. The Bishop of Rome sent to all the station-churches a bit of his own host, to be used in their individual sacrifice, and thereby to bind together in one the whole body of the faithful.

The meal of common fellowship, which in primitive days (as we have seen) was integrated into the sacrificial action after the pattern of the Last Supper, had been separated from that action because of abuses that came about through the wide dissemination of Christianity among Gentiles. For a time, it appears, the *agapè* was carried on as a separate function of the body of believers; but within a reasonably short period it practically dropped out of existence, although there seems little evidence for any specific step taken to put an end to the meal. Henceforward, the Eucharist itself was both the Christian offering or pleading of the redemptive work of Christ and also the occasion when Christians came together to express their 'love one of another.'

This was indeed singularly appropriate. For Christian faith, it was the redemptive work of Christ that had bound Christians into a new and wonderful unity. It was their conviction that (as Piers Plowman was later to have it)

> Blood brothers we became there,
> And gentlemen each one.

And if the social expression of fellowship in Christ was most appropriately a meal shared together, the Eucharist, even in its subsequent form with the supper eliminated and attention centered solely on the memorial of Christ himself, was the highest occasion for that expression. Here the bond of unity was established in a supremely telling manner. For here Christ—in whom the unity was grounded —was present, as the mystical Body of Christ pleaded his sacrifice for the sins of the world, a sacrifice by which the Christian community as a 'peculiar people' had come into existence. Those who were new creatures in Christ experienced the joy of the fellowship of the new creation when they met together to 'make Eucharist.'

Sufficient attention has now been given to this eucharistic *idea* of the early Church. The several points that have been mentioned provide the pattern for the subsequent development of the Church's thought and practice in worship. Here, as we have seen, is the central and particular action of the Christian Church, the normal and right way of Christian worship. It springs from the action of Christ himself at the Last Supper and is concerned with making *anamnesis* or memorial of the redemptive work that he accomplished and upon which at the Last Supper he set the seal of his own willing acceptance. As the central and expressive action of the Church, the Eucharistic Memorial has as its setting the conception of the Church as the Body of Christ, so that the sacrifice that is pleaded is the sacrifice that is indeed the life of the Church itself. 'Every member of the same' has his part and place in it. In the context of this offering, the true reality of Christ himself, in his humanity, is made present, so that the eucharistic elements become 'the body and blood of Christ,' to be received by the faithful; and this communion in Christ is linked with the offering of the sacrifice in such a fashion that the two are always seen as parts of a single action. Finally, through the common Eucharist the faithful realize their fellowship with one another as they are united with their Lord in pleading his redemptive work and receiving the strengthening holy food. Here is Christianity expressed in cult-act, as it is also expressed in the Church's faith and in the quality of life in Christ that marks those who are members of the Body.

In the *Apostolic Tradition* of Hippolytus we read that the early Christians brought with them tokens of their work, and not only the actual eucharistic elements of bread and wine, when they came to the weekly celebration. These were all offered and blessed, set apart, as it were, to God's use. The offertory was not a formality; it was the bringing of that which men had made or done or earned, so that it might serve as a symbol of their total personality offered to God. This sense of complete dedication to God was then carried back into the daily life of the believer, as he also took with him the consecrated element, with whose reception he would begin his day. Here is an aspect of the early Church's eucharistic life that later was almost entirely forgotten. Its recovery through the so-called 'liturgical movement' has been a momentous event in the life of the contemporary Church. Of this aspect of the Christian Sacrifice we shall have much to say later. We simply mention it at this point because it is so closely related to the whole question of the centrality of the Eucharist in the early Church and the participation of every Christian in this action as an essential and necessary part of Christian duty.

It has often been remarked that Christians in the days of persecution seem to have shown a strange unwillingness to forsake their meetings of worship. The reason for this determination must have been something other than the mutual help derived from a common meeting or spiritual communion with Christ. There was one reason, and one reason only which could bring these men and women together, often at great danger to their lives. They came together because they believed, as part of their Christian faith, that it was impossible to be a Christian without offering the sacrifice. The Eucharist was to them no mere *addendum* to their religious experience; it was the heart of

Christianity. They would have been prepared to say: No
Eucharist, no Christianity. The *anamnesis*, which, as they
believed, Christ had commanded, was the summing up and
the speaking forth of the whole meaning of Christianity. In
this they were at one with the implied teaching of the New
Testament, with St. Paul's insistence that the Lord's death
was to be 'shown,' and with St. John's affirmation that the
'bread of life' was given in this action 'unto life eternal.'
How then could they 'forsake the gathering of themselves
together'? To do so would be to notify the world, and their
fellow believers, that they had given up the faith and de-
serted the fellowship.

If ever there was an integral Christianity, it was in
the days of the early Christian Church. Here belief and
worship and action were one, bound together in the life of
the 'royal priesthood,' which was shared by each one of the
faithful. The whole intention and direction of their lives as
Christians, redeemed by Christ, was that this, their sacrifice
because it was Christ's sacrifice, might be 'good and acceptable unto the Lord God.' Here the meaning of Christian
discipleship was made plain; and it was singularly appropriate that the word chosen to indicate this rite of the Christians was the Latin *sacramentum*, originally employed in
Rome to describe the oath by which a Roman soldier swore
obedience and fealty. It was a religious bond that held the
early Christians together so that they knew themselves to
be, in the phrase used by one of them, a 'third race.' They
were a new and different people whose loyalty was directed
not to the Roman state or to the ethnic deities, but to the
Lord whom they met in their eucharistic fellowship, whose

sacrifice they shared at the Christian 'breaking of bread,' and whose name they were prepared to honor as they suffered persecution and martyrdom.

It was, indeed, the eucharistic action that held them together. Thus it is right that our transition from the days of early Christianity to the Eucharist in the life of the continuing Church should be precisely here—for it was in the thing done at the Last Supper, the thing done on Calvary, the thing done in the totality of the life and work of the Lord Jesus Christ, that the Christian Church found its salvation. All these were at bottom not many things but *one* thing, the self-oblation of Christ for men, the redemptive action of Christ for men, the establishment of the life in Christ in men. It was this one thing, this one action, which was the life of the Christian Church, the life of each member of the Church, and the life which might be described with utter truth as 'the life which was the light of men,' the 'life eternal, that they might know thee, the only God, and Jesus Christ whom thou hast sent.'

From the days of the early Church, roughly during the first three to four hundred years, the eucharistic doctrine developed steadily. It was a development that followed upon Christian life and experience rather than a rational and schematic exposition of the action. But it was in a straight line, so to say: the theological exposition was an attempt to express the persisting reality of the Church's 'life in Christ' in a fashion consistent with its historic origin in the records of the days of his flesh and with the apostolic witness in regard to the meaning of those original data.

In another book, *Christ and Christian Faith*, the

writer has attempted to show the way in which this process took place in the interpretation of the significance of Jesus himself; and in a second volume, *His Body the Church*, the principles have been carried further in a treatment of the Christian method of theological articulation. The point of view of the present study of the Eucharist depends on positions reached in these earlier volumes. Christianity takes its rise from historical events apprehended in faith as being the action of God for man's salvation. This complex of event and apprehension, first declared in dramatic and credal fashion was soon put forward in a minimal dogmatic form that sought to preserve the essential truth and meaning of the historical reality. Afterward came further developments of the implication of the initial dogmatic formulation, with such implementation and such peripheral doctrinal detail as were necessary or seemed desirable. The test of the validity and soundness of this development is its congruity with the primitive records contained in the New Testament; the Scriptures, in this way, serve, as the Thirty-Nine Articles say, to *prove* (i.e. 'test') all dogmatic and doctrinal statements.

Now in the matter of eucharistic doctrine, the position reached by the early Church was that the Lord's Supper is a sacrificial action, related closely to Calvary and its benefits; it is a communion in the life of the truly present Christ, who is God and Man; it is properly a means of adoration of God-in-Man, the Lord Jesus Christ, who is thus truly present in the sacrament. All of the more precise development since that period has been by way of restating, safeguarding, more clearly defining or more specifically expressing certain aspects of this total fact of Christian life in the Body of Christ. The story of this development has been traced in several significant books—from the strictly historical side in Darwell Stone's great work, *History of the Doctrine of the Holy Eucharist*, and from the interpretative side in Yngve Brilioth's study, *Eucharistic Faith and Practice*. Our own purpose has been to present the minimal material behind the development. For the Church in the early centuries of its existence, as it became conscious of itself and turned to a thoughtful consideration of those beliefs and practices that made its life in faith significant and fruitful, built upon the New Testament tradition and laid down certain lines for further growth. It was like the life history of every man. In his infancy, childhood, and early adolescence the general structural form that will be his for the remainder of his life is laid down, not for the purpose of restricting further growth, but as setting forth those lines along which growth may be consistent with his nature and revealing of his potentialities. Here is a conception that is both dynamic and structural; it is not a static orthodoxy but a living and life-giving orthodoxy, intent on persistence of type, but intent also upon adapting that type, without essential change of nature, to the new circumstances and conditions in which it must exist.

Precisely this process may be traced in eucharistic thought. The three structural elements are sacrifice, communion, and presence, held within a central action that is a true memorial of the redemptive work of the Lord Jesus Christ. To these matters we shall now turn our attention, first concerning ourselves with the Eucharist as 'Action,' and then moving on to the sacrificial nature, the communion, and the presence of Christ in the sacrament, all of them interrelated and interdependent, but for our purpose possible of discussion separately under these several heads.

4] *The Eucharist as Action*

During the New Testament period and in the days of the early Christian Church, the Christian Sacrifice was understood primarily as an action. We have seen that this sacrificial act of worship was the eucharistic memorial of the redemptive work of Christ, and that it was fashioned after the table meals of Judaism, with the additional but all-important and determinative significance given by the acts and words of Christ himself at the Last Supper. The essential element in the memorial was *that which was done;* it was not that which was present in the inspired consciousness of the worshippers, in their state of mind or their emotions. A *thing done* in the past was 'remembered'; a *thing done* by the Body of Christ was the means whereby the redemptive event on Calvary was made a present reality in the life of the Christian community.

⌈In our contemporary use of words like 'memory,' 'memorial,' or 'remembrance,' we tend to narrow the significance of the words to a *mental* situation. We remember something by entering, as it were, into a reverie, in which we return *in thought* to 'times long past.'⌋Or, if we *do* anything about what has occurred historically, it is by bringing back into our own minds, for meditation, the 'memory' of the occurrence. Even on such occasions as Memorial Day, Americans are concerned with a 'state of

mind,' which is brought into being by appropriate ceremonies and inspiring orations. The sense in which the words
'memory,' 'memorial,' and 'remembrance,' have been used
historically of the Christian Eucharist is very different from
this modern one. The difference is so great, indeed, that one
of the real difficulties in our discussion of the Eucharist is
that into our thinking on the subject there constantly ob-
trudes the modern idea of 'memorial,' which effectively
contradicts the notion that has been central to the entire
rite.

For the ancient Jews, 'to remember' meant something very strong and very real. The Passover, for example,
was the great Jewish feast of remembrance. But no Jew
would have thought that the feast was simply a turning
back *in mind* to meditate on the mighty acts in the past,
whereby God had delivered his ancestors from the Egyptians, had brought them through the Red Sea, and had established them as his chosen people in the Holy Land. That
would have been an artificial kind of memorializing. When
the devout Jew participated in the ceremonies and rites
associated with the Passover festival, he was re-calling the
mighty acts of Jahweh in a much more definite and vital
sense. He was acting on God's promise bringing out of the
past the total meaning, significance, value, and result of that
which God had done. He was *doing something*—as, for instance, eating in haste the Passover lamb—which brought to
bear on the immediate present of the Jewish nation what
God had accomplished for it in the past. He was lifted out
of the sheer contemporaneousness of the present moment
into a situation in the area we might well call, following

German theological discussion, *Heilsgeschichte*, or 'salvation-history'; it was a situation in which what had once been done became that which was now being done. The Passover, with all that it implies, was there with him, not because *he* chose to have it so, but because God had promised that when his faithful people 'remembered' his mighty acts, he would be with them as their Saviour, the God of the chosen people Israel.

The important point, then, in the memorial of the Passover was *that which was done*. We are not here concerned, of course, with the precise historicity (in the usual scientific sense of the word) of the stories the Jews told to account for their Passover festival. Doubtless the accounts we find in the Book of the Exodus are to a greater or less degree of the nature of etiological legend—stories told to explain and account for a certain rite or practice. Our concern is that the Jews of the time believed that these stories gave the origin of their festival, and that it was their profound conviction that these events had been the occasion of their peculiar choice as God's own people. So it was that when they held their Passover meal, with the ceremonies that always accompanied the festival, they believed that by the things done therein the God of Israel ratified and confirmed, through the actions done in obedience to his command, that which he had done once for all by the mighty deliverance of which the Passover spoke. It was not that they thought back upon what had been done, and praised God for it, although this was part of the total action. It was that God through their memorial made present and beneficial for his people that which God had done and for which they praised him. (Cf. Exodus 12:1-28, esp. vv. 24-7; and Deuteronomy 16:1-8.)

It is in this context that the Christian notions of 'memorial,' 'memory,' and 'remembrance' are employed in connection with the Lord's Supper. When the Anglican divines of the Caroline period spoke of the Eucharist as a 'sacrifice of commemoration,' they were using strictly proper language. The 'commemoration' is not a mental matter alone. It is not a question of 'I should like to have been with him then,' or of the kind of 'memorial' often associated with a Washington's Birthday Dinner.⌊It is a re-calling, a bringing into the present, of the actual *res gesta*, the things done by God in the mighty action in Christ whereby he brought salvation to the world.⌋We shall say more about the eucharistic sacrifice, in which the Christian community has found 'Calvary present still'; here we must emphasize that it is in the *action* of the Eucharist, not in thoughts stirred up in our minds or feelings awakened within us, that the memorial is to be found. This action is the meaning of the words in the Anglican canon, 'and in his holy gospel did command us to continue a perpetual *memory* of that his precious death and sacrifice . . .'

What, then, is the *action* that is the *memorial?*

The action in the Eucharist is complex in nature, as Dom Gregory Dix and others have pointed out. And this action, in its complex nature, goes directly back to the meals held by our Lord with his disciples, above all to the Last Supper, when the action was given its specific eucharistic and sacrificial significance. The words we may use to describe the action are those found in the evangelical record of the Last Supper, conveniently summarized in the tradition that St. Paul reports in First Corinthians and which the Anglican Prayer Book sets at the heart of the prayer of consecration: 'He *took* bread, and when he *had given thanks,* he *brake* it, and *gave* it to his disciples . . . He *took* the cup; and when he *had given thanks,* he *gave* it to them . . .'

The divisions in the eucharistic action, therefore, are these:

1. *The Taking*—which is the action that we should now indicate by the term 'offertory,' or the presentation of the elements of bread and wine for use in the sacrifice.

2. *The Giving Thanks*—which is the action we now call 'blessing' or 'consecration,' but which in the ancient Church would have been called the *eucharistizing,* or 'thanking over,' the bread and wine.

3. *The Breaking*—which is the fraction in later liturgies, and which of course can apply only to the bread, although the commingling of the fragment of bread with the wine in the chalice brings the wine into immediate connection with the action. This latter practice came into being through the custom established by the Bishop of Rome in uniting his Eucharist with those in the station-churches.

4. *The Giving*—which is the action now included in holy communion, during which the bread and wine, having been consecrated and hence having 'become' the 'Body and Blood of Christ,' are delivered to the faithful for them to receive as their holy food.

These four 'sub-actions' are aspects of the total action of the Eucharist. It is in the doing of these that the

Christian Sacrifice consists. But the eucharistic action is given its particular and peculiar *Christian* meaning by the fact that Christ at the Last Supper associated the taking, giving thanks, breaking, and giving with his own self-offering for the redemption of the world. It is that which he did—or, better, it is the fact that *he* did this—which makes the Eucharist what it is in the life of the Body of Christ. Christ in his mystical Body does that which Christ in the Upper Room performed. These are not two actions; they are one, since in each instance it is the one Christ who offers the sacrifice which is *his* sacrifice. In the first instance, it is offered *proleptically*, in the Upper Room; in the second instance, it is offered *memorially*, so that its benefits may be made available to the members of the mystical Body. In each instance it is the one sacrifice that is offered; and that is the sacrifice that historically was made once for all upon Calvary.

The Eucharist as memorial is *Action*. As we have said elsewhere, it is the 'Divine Action of the Body of Christ.' As such, it is the 'shewing forth' of the death of Christ, which is an inclusive term for the totality of his self-sacrifice. But as such, it is also the expressive act of the Church as the Body of Christ. We are likely to say, in speaking of some friend, that 'he is known by his actions.' So it is with the Church: it is known by its actions or, rather, by its Action, which is the memorial of the sacrifice of the death of Christ and the entrance into the benefits thereof. Less than this, the Christian Church can never claim, if it is to be true to the historical faith and to the witness of the primitive community. More than this it need not claim, for this is the Church's highest office: to plead by its action the death of Christ, thereby offering itself to God in *his* name and 'covered' by *his* offering, receiving back the holy food, which is for the 'strengthening and refreshing' of the members of the Body.

When our Lord, in connection with the fourfold action at the Last Supper, used such words as should forever associate broken bread and the shared cup with his redemptive work, he set upon the Eucharist the significance that the Christian fellowship, at first inchoately and later in more perfect apprehension, came to see was its essential meaning. We are therefore justified in asserting that while it is true that we do not have absolute scientific certainty in regard to these words, or unquestioned evidence that in the *historic human* mind of him who is also God such a development was explicitly ordered as in fact occurred, it is also true that the development was the means whereby the Church entered more deeply into the implicit and latent purpose and intention of the memorial. Further, it is a matter of right and reasonable faith, if one holds to the orthodox view of the person of Christ and the reality of the guidance of the Christian Church by the Holy Spirit, to say that this development of the primitive action into the full-orbed Christian Eucharist is the intention and purpose of the eternal Word of God and hence is part of his redemption. The Eucharist, that is to say, is integral to the action of Christ himself; indeed, we may consider with the late Paul Elmer More, that without the Eucharist the Christian understanding of the Incarnation and the Atonement is likely to be lost. In fact, one may say that it is almost certain to be lost.

We now return to the four divisions or 'sub-actions' in the Christian Sacrifice and shall consider each of them separately. We have seen that their total meaning is the Church's characteristic self-expression as the Body of Christ, in which Christ in the Church offers himself to the Father, not duplicating but pleading that which in Palestine he undertook for men. What is involved in and implied by the *taking, giving thanks, breaking*, and *giving?* How are they related to the life of the Church, to the individual believer, to the total faith of the Christian centuries? In what sense is *each* of them characteristic of the Christian tradition, its faith and life, as the *whole* action itself is characteristic of the tradition?

1. The Christian Sacrifice involves *taking*—that is, *offering*. In the eucharistic action the first step is necessarily the bringing of the elements that are to be used for the rite. These must be brought to the altar, so that they may be set apart for their new use, blessed, and given to the faithful. Traditionally, the bringing-up of the elements has been surrounded with great dignity and color. This was notably true in the primitive Church and persists to the present day in the Eastern Church, where the procession at the offertory is one of the high points in the entire service. The Western Church has tended to minimize the importance of this part of the Eucharist, although the *secreta* that are prescribed for the priest in the Roman mass indicate that nominally the offertory remains a highly important moment. Indeed, the language employed here in the Roman Church might seem to some to be more appropriate for use over the consecrated elements, since the phrases 'spotless

host' and 'chalice of salvation' appear to be more properly descriptive of the consecrated than of the unconsecrated bread and wine.

But the very fact that the language used at this point is of such a nature has its significance in the interpretation of the total eucharistic action. The truth is that the bread and wine that are presented at the altar, and that stand for the bread and wine that Jesus 'took' at the Last Supper, are already—even before the actual consecration—of the nature of 'holy objects.' They are being set apart by the very act of offering to the use and service of God. They are the token of the dedication of the worshippers to God, including in that dedication their souls and bodies, their lives and their deeds, their work and their play. Into the making of the bread and wine has gone the whole process of human endeavor. The bread and wine, therefore, are not 'bare tokens' but possess the meaning of the entire life of the faithful and by implication the entire world's work and life, as these are all offered to God. A thorough discussion of this side of the eucharistic action, with perhaps too strong a political emphasis but with an adequate treatment of the way in which the offertory represents the life of the worshippers and the world, is to be found in F. Hastings Smyth's *Discerning the Lord's Body*. Father Smyth points out that if the Eucharist be that which Christians have ever believed, the preparation of the elements for the Memorial is a matter of supreme importance, for into the elements that are offered go all the activities of those who bring them to the service, as well as the entire material world itself in so far as it contributes either directly or indirectly to the production and perfection of bread and wine. Hence every aspect of man's life is to be made worthy of the offertory, fit to be used as the instrumental medium through which the oblations are prepared. Where this worth and fitness cannot be found, life must be restored and redeemed by the intention of the Church that all should be dedicated to God.

The truth Father Smyth has stated is a necessary part of the understanding of the Action we are studying. The first movement in the Christian Sacrifice is the offering to God of the natural elements of human sustenance, bread and wine—appropriate since they are so ordinary and common. Into the preparation of these elements must go the devoted labor of the faithful—and by 'devoted' we mean given or dedicated to God, as in the sacrifices required of the Jews in the Old Testament.

It is regrettable that in the Western Church the symbolic value of the offertory has been forgotten or neglected. For here is the initial step in the Eucharist, and it is the step that must necessarily be made by the congregation. The bread and wine that are 'taken' are the bread and wine that must be offered, exactly as the elements Jesus Christ used at the Last Supper had first to be brought to the Upper Room before they could, in that evangelical action, be 'taken' and then blessed.

In summary we may say that the first aspect of the total eucharistic action is the offering of the natural elements of bread and wine, brought by the congregation, as a token and surrogate of their dedication of themselves and their entire lives to God, symbolizing and representing the world as it is returned to its Creator. Furthermore, the offertory is the action of the Church of Christ itself, as the Church is offered back to God, in and through the natural elements it presents. Here Christ in the Church takes the prepared bread and wine, standing for both the redeemed community and for the life of the world, and offers them to the Father in association with his own life and work. The redemptive action of God in Christ includes within itself the Church and the natural creation, of which the bread and wine are the particular things singled out to be used for a life-giving work.

2. *The Giving Thanks.* As we have seen it, it was customary among the Jews to set apart objects for holy use by saying a prayer of thanksgiving or a 'grace.' There was no direct blessing or consecration of objects in and for and of themselves; they were blessed or consecrated by some formula in which the God of Israel was himself thanked for having given them for the use and service of men. Hence the formulae at the Jewish table meals were of the nature of thanksgivings: 'Blessed be thou, O Lord God of creation, who bringest forth bread from the earth'; 'Blessed be thou, O Lord God of creation, who dost create the fruit of the vine.' Such formulae, or variants of them, were habitual in all Jewish table fellowship; direct blessings were unknown. So it is that the 'giving of thanks' is a crucial element in the Christian Sacrifice.

It is one of the most unfortunate of many unfortunate historical accidents that the Canon of the Mass in the Western Church has been marked ever since the early Middle Ages, as beginning with the prayer *Te Igitur;* and consequently, in the Anglican Prayer Books, the rubric indicates that the 'Prayer of Consecration' commences with words that in the American Prayer Book are: 'All glory be to thee, Almighty God . . .' For the truth is that the consecration in the Eucharist, which is the 'giving of thanks' over bread and wine in the name of Christ, following his example, according to his command, and with his intention, begins with the dialogue that in the liturgy opens with 'Lift up your hearts.' The specially significant words in this dialogue are 'Let us give thanks unto our Lord God.' For these words, running into the *Sanctus*, in which God is praised for his natural creation, go directly into a great thanksgiving for the redemption of the world by the Incarnate Son, and include as a specific part in, and a continuation of, that redemption the fact that 'in the night in which he was betrayed, he took bread . . .' The remainder of the prayer, as a careful reading will show, is a carrying on of this thanksgiving, until we reach the Trinitarian doxology near the close, 'through Jesus Christ our Lord, by whom, and with whom, in the unity of the Holy Ghost, all honour and glory be unto thee, O Father almighty, world without end.' And it ends with the eucharistic *Amen*, which is the *Our Father*, said by priest and people together. The worshippers rightly conclude their thanksgiving with the words taught by Christ himself as appropriate when men 'are bold' to approach their Creator.

The thanksgiving in the Christian Sacrifice, however, is different from that in the Jewish meal. For the Christian is bound to give thanks not only for the naturally good things of life, of which the bread and wine are symbols, but also for the redemption of the world by Christ—

and that means that the Christian thanks God for suffering and death, as well as for Incarnation, triumphant Resurrection, and Ascension. This is the unique and peculiar fact that distinguishes Christianity from all other religions. It is superbly illustrated in T. S. Eliot's play, *Murder in the Cathedral*, where the Christmas sermon of St. Thomas Becket is preached on the passion and death of Christ. Good Friday is linked with the Nativity, as the risen Lord of Easter Day is known in terms of the crucified Lord of Calvary. This is to say that the life of Christ is a totality, a single event, a 'seamless robe,' rather than a series of discrete incidents. It is also to say that in the very conditions that for men are the occasion of deepest pain and distress, the Christian is enabled by his faith in the divine work of God in Christ to see the reality of triumphant love not merely in spite of, or after, or as the reversal of, that which is painful and frustrating, but in and under the very pain and frustration themselves.

Thus the Christian thanksgiving is no mere optimism, but a deeply penetrating affirmation of the essential goodness of life and creation, redeemed by God as well as created by him. It is a theological assertion of the first importance, directly stated in liturgical fashion and vividly placarded before the faithful on each occasion that they assist in the pleading of the Christian Sacrifice.

The fact that the 'eucharistizing' of the bread and wine is in the tradition of the Jewish meals, and that it is the constant element in all the known forms of Christian eucharistic worship, as the word 'eucharist' itself indicates, has peculiar significance, for it answers the question of the means of consecration in the Lord's Supper. To ask 'What particular *words* effect the blessing in the table meal?' would have been meaningless to a Jew of the first century. In the early days of the Christian Church, it is likely that a similar question, framed along specifically Christian lines, would have been equally meaningless. The consecration in the Eucharist was effected by no special formula, by no particular set of words—certainly not by the recitation of the phrases that tradition reported had been used by Christ himself at the Last Supper, and probably not by the invocation of the Holy Spirit—but by the total *action*. Bread and wine were taken; they were set apart for use by a prayer in which God was thanked for them and for the redemptive work of Christ with which they were, by his own use, forever associated in this rite; and they were then distributed to the faithful who had gathered to 'remember' their Lord. That whole act was the consecration.

This will explain why in one of the ancient liturgies the so-called 'words of institution' are not found. They were evidently thought to be not needed, in the sense in which later Western theology thought they were necessary. The highly important and absolutely essential aspect of the Christian Sacrifice was the action itself, the taking and blessing and breaking and giving, rather than a set of words. Again, the evidence for the invocation of the Holy Spirit as an important, but still not essential, part of the consecration is very early; and some have held that it is earlier than the evidence for the 'words of institution.' But, once again, there is no trace of a belief that this invocation was in itself the necessary consecratory formula until a much later period in the Eastern Church.

What has been said in the foregoing paragraphs is not intended to deny the importance of the words of Christ at the Last Supper, repeated in the course of the eucharistic action. Neither is it intended to say that the *epiclesis*, or invocation of the Holy Spirit, is valueless. Both of these are central parts of the total action, as the Church has finally developed its liturgical usage. Nor is it necessarily the case, as some feel, that the ceremonial actions that in the Western Church have become attached to the 'words of institution' are simply corruptions. We may choose to think, if we are concerned with liturgical development, that the Anglican Church might work out a ceremonial entirely consistent with its prayer of consecration, rather than continue the borrowing that has been our recent practice. But in any event it remains true that the human mind tends to function in terms of times and places; and in those terms, there is no particular time or moment more climactically significant than the time or moment when Christ's words and actions, together, are dramatically repeated in the Eucharist. There is a possibility that we may let the here-and-now reality of the presence of Christ in the sacrifice evaporate into a sheer spirituality belonging to a kind of 'never never land,' unless there is some given point in the rite—either at the 'words of institution' or at the end of the eucharistic canon—at which we can say, 'Christ is *now* present with us in his sacrifice, under the eucharistic species of bread and wine.'

But the fact that this is so, and that if we are aware of human frailty, we shall be foolish to wish it otherwise, does not mean that we are to insist, *theologically*, that the particular words, 'This is my Body' and 'This is my Blood,' in and of themselves consecrate the elements. It is the *theological* side with which we have been concerned; and in that respect it must be clear that the *total* eucharistic action is the consecration. The particular moment in which bread is broken and the cup blessed has *its* meaning in the totality of the action, as one of the things Christ himself did, while the words have their importance in that they give Christ's own interpretation to that which the action, both as a whole and in each of its aspects, signifies and effects.

3. 'He brake it.' In these words, the action of Christ at the Last Supper, in which he presided as Master, is linked with the death he accomplished on the next day. What Jesus said in the Upper Room, as he performed the customary duty of the master of the table, set its seal upon what he did for men, when he gave his life as 'a ransom for many.' We have indicated that the Christian thanksgiving includes the death of Christ. The breaking of the body of Christ is represented not in a figure but in adumbrated reality at the Last Supper and in true 'memorial' (in the Jewish sense) whenever the Christian Church, taking bread, breaks it after the manner in which Christ himself broke it in the Upper Room. Not in a figure, we just said; yet it *is* in a figure, if by that we mean in an action that does not repeat but yet makes present a reality once for all accomplished. For a traditional name of the Eucharist is 'the breaking of bread,' which is a way of saying 'the memorial of the breaking of the body of Christ on Calvary.' Without that breaking, there would have been no salvation in the sense

in which Christians employ the term and know the thing
for which it stands.

The breaking of bread was for the Jewish people a
part of their customary religious table fellowship. There is
a certain significance in the action quite apart from anything that our Lord himself said or did. To eat bread taken
from a common loaf, broken that it may be shared, speaks
much about men's participation one with another in a life
that requires give and take, sacrifice, and mutual help. One
of the old Italian noble families has preserved for centuries
a similar rite. Once a year the members of the family and
their servants regularly participate. This ceremony shows
a sense of the common bond established by the breaking of
bread together. But for the Christian there is more than this.
The bread which he breaks is 'the communion of the body
of Christ,' as the cup which he shares is 'the communion of
the blood of Christ.' It is *Christ's* life that is partaken of
and shared in the Christian meal of fellowship, not simply
the good will and sacrifice that is found when men gather
together or find a common bond in some human association
of blood or cause.

The Christian Church is the Body of Christ. As its
expressive rite, it takes the elements that are the natural
goods of the world of God's creation; it thanks the elements
into the 'body and blood of Christ'; and then it breaks the
bread that is Christ's body and, by association with that
breaking, shares the common cup. Here the eucharistic
bread, which becomes the body of Christ sacramentally
present, is broken, as the bread was broken by Christ; the
two are one, and both are identified with the breaking of

Christ's body on the Cross of Calvary. What is more, they
are one with the breaking of the life of the Body of Christ
which is the Church, self-offered to the Father in service
to men and in surrender to God. This is the mystery of the
identification of the mystical Body which is the Church
with the eucharistic body of the Lord; and the unity of
both of these is in their identification with the body of
Christ once offered on Calvary for the sins of the world.
Highly imaginative as this may sound, it is, for those who
have entered into the Christian secret, no matter of words
alone, but the profound reality of their experience in the
en-Christed life of the Body of Christ. It is part of the
eucharistic action. Like every part of the action, it is a part
in which the members of the Body of Christ share, not only
as it is performed in their presence and with their assistance,
but as it is they themselves, in the person of their Head,
who are 'taken' and 'thanked over' and 'broken.' It is they
themselves, their lives and their labors, who are given to
God in union with Christ and in Christ, so that they may
receive their significance and intention for living from him.

4. The *Giving*. The final step in the eucharistic
action is the communion, when those who are 'very members incorporate in Christ's mystical Body' are fed with the
holy food that is the life of Christ himself. The Christian
Sacrifice is one in which those who assist are also those who
participate; it is not an 'external' ceremony, but one that
demands and implies communion with the Lord in his sacrifice.

At the Last Supper itself, the bread and wine that
had been taken and blessed were shared by the disciples,

after the Master of the table fellowship had associated the
elements with his death, which was to be accomplished the
next day. The traditional words used with the cup make
this quite plain: 'This cup is the new covenant in my blood.'
By participation in the eucharistic elements, the salvation
of Christ, which was the new covenant in his blood, was
known and shared and entered into by the faithful. And
this was traced back to the scene in the Upper Room, when
the Lord himself, before his death, had brought his 'little
flock' into the new covenant by their sharing in the meal
that was an adumbration of the messianic meal to be held
in the Kingdom of God, when that kingdom should come.
So the early Church believed. Hence the completion of the
eucharistic action is the communion of the faithful. Hence,
too, no offering of the Christian Sacrifice has ever been regarded as right unless at least some communions are made
—even in High Mass today, where usually very few if any
of the congregation are expected to communicate, the
Western Church has insisted that at least the celebrant must
make his communion, so that the action of the Eucharist
may be complete.

The liturgy of the Anglican Communion, in its several forms, is quite explicit here, since it envisages no offering of the Eucharist without at least the opportunity for
general congregational participation. It is communion *in the
sacrifice*—for the Anglican liturgy is very heavily weighted
on the sacrificial side, as the catechism indicates when it
mentions the purpose of the service as simply 'the continual
remembrance of the sacrifice of the death of Christ, and of
the benefits which we receive thereby.' But the general

communion is plainly intended, at least as an opportunity. The Anglican Communion has maintained a balance in the Eucharist that has been lost in certain other parts of the Western Church.

What, then, is *given* by Christ and received by the faithful in the eucharistic action? It is the body and blood of Christ. That is to say, it is the holy food that is Christ's own life, made available by Christ himself for those who are members of his Body the Church. 'He gives himself by his own hand.' It is he who took bread, gave thanks for it, brake it, and then gave it to the disciples; so it is he who took his life which he had prepared for the Father as an offering, dedicated it to God in self-sacrifice, and let it be broken upon the Cross, and who now in the fellowship of his people returns that life to them for 'the strengthening and refreshing of their souls,' to the end that they 'may live in him, and he in them.' In a later chapter we shall undertake a consideration of the precise theological meaning of the words, 'the body and blood of Christ'; it is sufficient here to indicate that the Christian Church has always meant by these something real and ontological, rather than a conventional figure or a convenient metaphor. That by which the faithful are fed is the true life of Christ, incarnate and crucified and risen and ascended. It is the life that was offered by him when, in the Upper Room, he 'gave it to his disciples.' In the historic scene it was present implicitly, until he should have accomplished his death; in the day-by-day offering of the Christian Sacrifice, it is present in fact, given at the altars of the Church to the members of the Body.

Once again, it is necessary to remark that even though we may not find this full sense of the Christian Eucharist in the human mind of Jesus, so far as we can read that mind, it is obvious that once the orthodox understanding of the Incarnation and the reality of the Church's guidance by the Holy Spirit are accepted, the record of what transpired in the Upper Room and the Church's developing insight into the eucharistic action fit into a pattern that is perfectly plain and comprehensible. Questions in regard to the way in which Christ's body and blood were present on the table at the Last Supper are then seen to be beside the point. The historical situation and the historical development fall into place. The mind and work of Christ, historic and human on the one hand, and eternal and divine on the other, are seen with each nature in its right relation to the other. The historic Lord, with his historic limitations, did that which was *required* to be done if the purpose of the eternal Word to provide for men the true sacrificial action and the true 'supersubstantial' food was to be effected. If 'types and shadows' were to 'have their ending,' it must be in that rite which fulfilled and corrected them. As the Epistle to the Hebrews has shown, it is Christ who does this fulfilling and correcting, in his historical manifestation. The 'newer rite,' in which man's desire for sacrificial communion with the Reality to whom he owes his being and from whom he seeks salvation shall find its perfect realization, is this eucharistic action. Here the 'bread of heaven' is given to men.

There are, then, four parts in the Christian Action: offering, thanksgiving, fraction, and communion. Each one is essential to the whole, both in our understanding of what actually took place in the Upper Room and in our apprehension of the rite in which 'a continual remembrance' of Christ's redemptive work is made. Every known liturgy possesses these four parts in some form, whether it be the most primitive and undeveloped rite or the fully rounded liturgical orders found in East and West, in 'Orthodox' and 'Catholic' communions, and in the worship of those groups originating at the time of the Reformation. Sometimes, these liturgies may be altered from the sequence we discover in general early usage; but the four parts are there, and their proper performance has always been regarded as necessary to a fully authenticated and properly certified offering of the Eucharist as the Christian Sacrifice.

When the Prayer Book of the Episcopal Church uses the words, 'we do celebrate and make,' of the Eucharist, it is following the principle upon which our discussion in these pages has been based—the principle that the Christian service of worship is something *done*, something 'made' by the faithful of the Church before God and man, not an 'interior' or 'spiritual' memorial. Baron von Hügel remarked on one occasion that monism is the most dangerous enemy of Christianity. This statement is certainly true, but there is another enemy that is almost as dangerous as monism. It is 'spirituality' at the expense of the materiality that belongs to life; a kind of Neoplatonic 'mentalism' that evaporates religion into a state of mind supposed to supplant all the 'crude' and 'magical' and 'superstitious' rites and ceremonies with which religion has been historically associated.

This idea, prevalent in our own day not only among

the 'religiously minded' who are unattached to any institutional religion, but also among many who are professing Christians, is vastly different from the religion that for two thousand years has borne the name of Christianity. *That* religion, for good or bad, is tied down to historical events, with all their contingency. It is tied down to flesh and blood, in the focusing of its faith on One who although he is believed to be God is also believed surely to be Man. It is tied down to material elements in that it is through tangible, visible things like bread and wine and water that it finds its normal avenue of approach to God. It is tied down to things done in plain and obvious fashion, such as taking bread and wine, saying words of thanksgiving over them, breaking or sharing them, and then eating and drinking them. In this last set of actions Christianity, as historically known, has concentrated its life in worship: in making this Memorial, Christ, the Redeemer who is God-in-Man, continues his work of reconciliation through his Body the Church.

It is perfectly conceivable that Christianity, in this historical sense, is untrue. That is a question thoughtful men must consider. But if Christianity is true at all, in any recognizable sense of the term 'Christian,' *this* is the Christianity which is true. If we acknowledge its truth, then we are bound also to recognize and acknowledge the integrity of the Christian *thing*, which involves a faith believed because a deed was done, an act of worship that is an action continuous with the Lord's own action and informed by the significance implicit in that action. Christian worship, in other words, is simple obedience to the command that the

early Church believed to have been given by Christ himself: 'Do this in remembrance of me.')

    We have sufficient assurance that Christ's intention
was to initiate his disciples into the results that his self-
offering would bring about. That is a minimum, perhaps;
it is enough, however, to explain the Christian Church's
emphasis on the 'breaking of bread' in Christ's remembrance.
Some of us may be able to feel a great degree of certainty
about the earliest records; some of us may have less certainty about the records. The one thing that is utterly sure
is that no conclusions of Biblical criticism and no study of
the primitive days of the Christian Church can deny the
fact that the eucharistic action of the Body of Christ is continuous with the action of Christ at the Last Supper or with
the intention that was there given. In this continuity we
may rest content. Obviously, a critic who approaches the
records with a bias against the kind of religion that Christianity has been shown historically to be may see something
else in the story. But it is his presuppositions, and not the
historical evidence, that will explain his reading of events.
For us, writing from within the Catholic community that
itself preserved the records, the conclusion is expressed in
Thomas Aquinas's moving words: *God, who under a wonderful sacrament didst leave unto us a memorial of thy Passion, grant us so to venerate the sacred mysteries of thy
Body and Blood, as evermore to perceive within ourselves
the fruits of thy redemption, who livest and reignest with
the Father and the Holy Ghost, world without end. Amen.*

5] *The Eucharist as Sacrifice*

The title that has been given this book was chosen with no controversial thought in mind. From at least as early as the *Didache* in the first half, and perhaps even the first quarter, of the second century, the Eucharist has been regarded as the Christian 'equivalent' of the sacrificial worship of Judaism and of the non-Jewish religions. In the Catechism of the Book of Common Prayer of the Episcopal Church, it is asserted that the primary significance of this Christian sacramental rite is of a sacrificial nature: 'the continual remembrance of the sacrifice of the death of Christ.' Furthermore, as we have already indicated in the second chapter, St. Paul gives this description of the nature of the Eucharist, when he says that the Lord's Supper is the way in which 'ye do shew forth the Lord's death.'

Worship in the period during which the Christian Eucharist came into being was of a sacrificial character, both for the Jewish people and among the Gentiles. The worship in the synagogue, often cited as an instance of definitely non-sacrificial worship, is, in truth, not a case in point. It was a surrogate for Temple worship, developed during the exile, when the Jews were unavoidably prevented from participating in the sacrifices of the central sanctuary in Jerusalem, and continued after the return from the exile as ancillary to Temple worship, but never as a

substitute for it. A Jew of the first century, while most of
his actual experience of worship might have been obtained
in the predominantly instructional service of the synagogue,
would have answered immediately, if the question had been
put to him, that this synagogue service was as nothing in
comparison with the action of the whole people of Israel,
who offered, through their designated priestly agents in the
Holy City, the worship that was supremely acceptable to
God. It is correct to say with Dr. Gavin (in his *Jewish
Antecedents of the Christian Sacraments*) that the atmosphere in which the Eucharist came into being as the distinctive mode of worship for those who were members of
the Christian community was such that a sacrificial character would inevitably and without question be ascribed
to their peculiar rite. It is also true that the Christian notion
of sacrifice and the way in which it was offered would
differ, and did differ, from the conventionally accepted
one, inasmuch as the new faith was in its orientation and
outlook different from the older religions. Yet even here
it is important to emphasize that although there were differences, there were resemblances. Professor Nock has
made out a good case for his contention that Christianity
conquered the world by being the most appealing instance
of the general orientation that the mystery religions, later
on, were to attempt to satisfy. Nor should this be regarded
as a condemnation of the early preaching and practice of
Christianity, unless we have imported into our study presuppositions that make any idea of sacrifice or sacrament
an alien intrusion into a 'simple Galilean gospel.'

    The Christian Eucharist, therefore, must be said to

be in some genuine sense 'the Christian Sacrifice.' So it has ever been considered; so it is now considered by the vast majority of Christians. So it must indeed be considered if due regard is given to its origins, its association by Christ's own action with Calvary, and its benefits as these have been understood and received by the generality of Christian worshippers. We wish now to see in what sense the eucharistic action is a sacrifice. In what sense is it that which the Prayer Book plainly calls it, 'a perpetual memory of that his precious death and sacrifice'? A *memorial*, in the Jewish and primitive meaning of that term—yes; an *action*, in that it concerns something done, and is itself a 'doing'—yes. How, then, are these related to a sacrificial offering?

The first question to be answered, of course, is the meaning of the term 'sacrifice.' Etymologically, it appears to signify 'the making holy' that is brought about by some ritual action. In religious practice, sacrifice has come to mean the offering of some valuable object or objects to a divine being, so that blessings and benefits may be secured. The sacrifice may be on a very 'low' level, as we say; on the other hand it may be very 'high' indeed. The benefits sought may be purely material, such as better crops, protection from an enemy, good weather, and so on; on the other hand, they may be such developed and moralized benefits as increase in divine favor, strengthening to do the will of God, or communion with the deity who is being invoked. Whichever of these kinds of offering may be in mind and whatever benefits may be desired, the fact remains that sacrifice in some form appears to be practically universal among men.

So soon as the human race came to a belief in supernatural Reality, whether that was thought of in polytheistic or in unitary ways, just so soon the desire to make an offering to the god or gods made its appearance. Anthropologists have pretty well established this. R. R. Marett, for instance, in his careful studies of primitive religion that appeared under the title *Sacraments of Simple Folk*, has shown conclusively the presence of sacramental religion at the early stages of human development, at least so far as science can determine. And the manner in which this sacramentalism is expressed is, as Marett has indicated, by an offering made to the god of the tribe or place.

Indeed, it might be suggested that from one point of view the religious history of man is nothing other than the story of his search for a satisfactory way of offering sacrifice to the divine Reality, however imperfectly he may have pictured that Reality. Frequently, in primitive times, the kind of offering he made was horrible in the extreme. The slaying of the firstborn of a tribe or the practice of human sacrifice in other forms—as in the offering of the most beautiful girl of a clan or the mutilation of a young warrior, with crude attendant rites—seems to us ghastly and barbaric. So they both are. But to primitive man they were a way of recognizing the all-compelling claims of his god, a being who was so great and exalted that if the sacrifice were to be worthy of him, he must be given the best that man had to give. As the race became more sophisticated, more sensitive to moral values, more discerning in its apprehension of the nature of the divine Reality, the cruder kinds of sacrifice gave place to others of a more refined nature.

The firstborn of the flock took the place of the firstborn son of the tribe. Offerings of grain and fruit were made, instead of offerings of human life. But these offerings were still the token of that dedication to the will of the divine being which is behind the entire sacrificial idea.

To suppose that the savage, as we gratuitously call him, was concerned simply with his own advantage in the offering of his sacrifices shows very little insight. On the contrary, there was present in his 'savage breast' some dim apprehension of the truth of the sovereignty of God, grasped under very inadequate and perhaps even perverse symbols and images, but none the less redeeming his exist-ence from the sheerly animal or solely human level by plac-ing it in relation to some supernatural Reality that could and did make demands upon his life and offer him, in time of need, a genuine succor.

The highest level that has been reached in the realm of human dedication to God is found, for the greatest num-ber of people in a given race or nation, among the Jews. Through the work of great priests and prophets, the Jewish conception of the meaning of sacrificial action had been so purified and refined that, by the time of the coming of Christ, there was left in it little that was barbaric and super-stitious. Those who have some congenital prejudice against all sacrificial ideas may disagree at this point; the proof that they have misunderstood is shown by the simple fact that the One who was the teacher of the most 'spiritual' of all religions did not himself criticize or condemn the sac-rificial system of the Jewish people, but actually took part in it. What he did denounce was the abuse of the sacrificial cult, as when money-changers extorted their charges from the poor, or when the priests and others who maintained the cult failed to recognize that mercy and sacrifice in the moral sense were to have precedence over ceremonial, since the man who offers the sacrifice must be one who is worthy to offer it, or must be made worthy. But the view that the Temple offering was wrong or that the idea of sacrifice was pernicious cannot be found anywhere in the teachings of Jesus Christ.

The sacrifices of the Jewish Temple however, were not sufficient. The author of Hebrews makes this the heart of his appeal. 'The blood of bulls and of goats, and the ashes of a heifer sprinkling the unclean' are indeed said by him to purify those to whom they are applied, according to the pattern of the sacrificial offering in the Temple. Yet they are efficacious only in that they are figures or hints of the one sacrifice which alone can take away sin, as they are also figures or hints of the one sacrifice which is acceptable to God because it is worthy of him. That sacrifice is made when a man says, 'Lo, I come to do thy will, O God.' To offer oneself, soul and body, to God is the perfect sacrifice; it does not negate or deny the other token sacrifices but brings out their proper intention in the history of religion. What God wishes from men, if he be the God in whom the Hebrew tradition has believed, is simply themselves, in token of which they can and do and should make other sacrifices that are never *substitutes* for themselves but are the human way of indicating that they do indeed offer themselves.

This is the very thing, however, that man cannot

do, of and by himself. If he could do this, the removal of his self-isolation from God would be brought about and he would be in free communion with his Creator. That free fellowship with his Creator would be the great benefit of the perfect sacrifice of self to God. But man is a sinner. Even at his best, he is not worthy of God, because he fails to realize the nature that belongs to him as creature of God. This failure is called theologically 'original sin.' Man, in other words, is not really man; he is fallen from the potential perfection that belongs to him, and hence he knows that he is not worthy of the God who demands that the offering shall be perfect *of its kind*. What is more, man does not even have the capacity totally and fully to offer himself to God. If he is in original sin, as an actual fact of his life, he is also possessed by concupiscence, as theology calls it—that is, he has a tendency to secure his own immediate satisfaction, and is thereby prevented from giving himself unreservedly to the highest that he knows. This is man's dilemma. On the one hand, he wants to offer himself to God in perfect, obedient service; on the other, he cannot offer and he refuses to offer himself to God in this fashion.

The Christian faith sees Jesus Christ as the answer to man's dilemma. God alone can provide for man the sacrifice that is perfect. The sacrifice as we have seen, would be a completely dedicated life: 'Lo, I come to do thy will, O God.' Man cannot offer this; but God in Man, God as Man, can and does make this offering. That is the meaning of the life of Christ. This is why à Kempis can call the whole life of Jesus *mysterium crucis*. Perfect obedience to God in a life perfectly offered to him—here is perfect sacrifice. It is this to which the ancient sacrifices pointed, but which they were unable to fulfil. It is this that not only the Jewish but the Gentile sacrificial ceremonies, the primitive and barbaric as well as the refined and spiritual rites, were prefiguring and implying. The 'types and shadows' were *real* types and *real* shadows, not mere wickedness and error and perversion. Christ is the perfection of that for which they were seeking and which, in some dim way, they actually declared.

But the perfect obedience of a life entirely offered to God is not the whole story. For that life included the Cross. In the circumstances of Judaism, at the particular time and place in which he lived during the days of his flesh, Jesus brought within the ambit of the sacrifice the 'brokenness' of life. It is not merely that a good life is offered to God. The profound truth is that the good life which this human world in itself could not contain or support, because that good life is too good for sinful men, was offered to God in sacrifice to the point of death and in fullest obedience, when such was its manifest and inevitable destiny. Humanly speaking, the Jewish people crucified the Lord; from the standpoint of eternal providence, God by this action took into himself the suffering of men, their frustration and their sin. By accepting it as part of the good life of perfect obedience which the incarnate Lord offered to the Father, he redeemed men and gave them new life. The new life was *in Christ;* it was by sharing in *his* victory that they might achieve their victory, or, rather, that he might achieve victory in them. The Cross is the culmination of Christ's life of obedience; as St. Bernard said, 'not the death itself, but the willingness of the One who died' is the sacrifice of Calvary. Yet Calvary, as life given to the point of death, is the necessary completion of the sacrifice of Christ, if there is to be offered to the divine Reality the fullness of human life, in its every range and every aspect.

At the Last Supper Christ by his own action identified the eucharistic action with his self-offering to the Father. With his intention to accept the fate before him, thereby turning it from fate to high destiny, he made his death a sacrifice that he would offer for men. If he did not say it, it is certainly implicit in his action that he intended this to be the giving of his life as a ransom for many. To ask 'Ransom *from what?*' is to betray a failure to understand the Jewish idiom of the time. A 'ransom' was a sacrifice or price given that men might be free; it was not necessary to work out details of the transaction, as if it were some business operation, requiring a contract signed, sealed, and delivered, with witnesses and other legal technicalities. Furthermore, Jesus in the Upper Room made the sacrificial death of the next day a reality associated with the broken bread and the shared cup. 'This is my body, broken for you.' 'This is the new covenant in my blood.' His death was a sacrifice. By it, there would be established in a final sense a relationship or covenant between God and men that would write God's law in their hearts, would free them from sin to be possessors of the liberty of God's children, and would open to them the Kingdom of Heaven.

Hence the Last Supper was a proleptic sharing in a sacrifice that was to be accomplished. And the Lord's Supper, which the Christian Church continued to celebrate as its characteristic action, is the entrance by 'commemoration' into the sacrifice that was in fact made on Good Friday. As such, it is the showing forth of Christ's death; it is the pleading of the redemptive work of Christ; it is a participation in the benefits of that redemptive action, as by communion the members of the Church dwell in Christ and he in them. So the Lord's Supper, the Christian 'Thanksgiving,' is sacrificial in nature. It is the Christian Sacrifice, for it is the continuation and the implementation, in the mystical Body of Christ which is the Church, of the 'one oblation of himself once offered' in his physical body on the Cross. Christ is one, and wherever he gives himself to the Father or to his human brethren, it is the same Christ who is doing the same thing for the same purpose in the same way. 'The newer rite' of Christian worship is a sacrifice, but not of 'the blood of bulls and of goats'; it is the entrance of the mystical Body of Christ into the sacrifice of Christ, which is the mystery of the Church's own being.

One of the prevalent misunderstandings of the meaning of sacrifice as applied to the Christian Action is that this notion must inevitably involve some superstitious or magical attempt to influence God in the interests of the one who offers the sacrifice. It is obvious that such a danger plagues all religion; yet it is equally clear that the distinction between magic and religion is overwhelming. Magic is the attempt to coerce the powers that govern the world into doing one's own will; religion is the desire to offer oneself so that one may be an obedient instrument of the divine purpose. Now the entire significance of the Christian Sacrifice is in the conforming of the worshipper to the will and purpose of God, by bringing him into communion with divine Reality through the mediation of Christ and by means of Christ's perfect sacrifice. The essence of the Christian sacrificial notion is found in the words of William Bright,

> Look, Father, look on his anointed face,
> And only look on us as found in him.

The most evangelical Protestant will heartily agree with this sentiment; it is only as 'found in Christ' that we can make any claims upon God's mercy. What the critic fails to see is that the Eucharist as sacrifice is not a substitute for the perfect sacrifice of Calvary, as if there were anything lacking in the utter completeness of that act of Christ's. It is not a substitute for or a sacrifice in addition to Calvary; it is, rather, an entrance into and a pleading of 'the merits' of that sacrifice, made possible because the Church is the mystical Body of the Lord and thereby can make that sacrifice its own. The Church is enabled to make its sacrificial action identical with the once-for-all event on Calvary because it is the same Christ who offered himself on Calvary and who gives himself in his Body the Church.

Furthermore, the 'repetitive' notion so strongly—and so rightly—condemned in the Anglican Thirty-Nine Articles (where it is declared that 'sacrifices of Masses, in the which it was commonly said, that the priest did offer Christ for the quick and the dead, to have remission of pain or guilt' are 'blasphemous fables and dangerous deceits') is without doubt unchristian. For what 'was commonly said' was that the repeated offering of the sacrifice was by way of adding additional merit to Calvary, so that 'the more masses said, the more reward given.' The offering of the Eucharist for the quick and the dead, that they may enter more nearly into communion with God through Christ, is right and proper; the assumption that the Eucharist will 'buy off' the sinner from 'pain or guilt' is indeed both 'blasphemous' and 'dangerous.'

The Article we have quoted begins with a thoroughly sound and admirably terse statement of the fundamental theological presupposition for any Christian sacrificial notion of the Eucharist: 'The offering of Christ once made is that perfect redemption, propitiation, and satisfaction, for all the sins of the whole world, both original and actual; and there is none other satisfaction for sin, but that alone.' Precisely. The Eucharist is a sacrifice because it is that 'offering of Christ once made,' herein pleaded and offered to the Father, set between 'our sins and their reward.'

> We here present, we here spread forth to thee
> That only offering perfect in thine eyes,
> The one, true, pure, immortal sacrifice.

But it is no *new* sacrifice that is being set forth, presented, or pleaded. It is Christ's sacrifice, for that sacrifice alone avails.

This is the evangelical note that is at the heart of true Catholic eucharistic piety. It is extraordinary that this has not always been noticed by critics. Yet John and Charles Wesley, whose evangelical concern is beyond question, wrote their most moving hymns about the sacrifice of Christ in connection with the Eucharist. They recognized what should be evident to any discerning student; they saw that despite perversions and errors, the evangelical truth is still there. It is found in the official Roman liturgy and, much more patently, in the eucharistic offices in the Anglican Prayer Books.

In recent years, a distinguished French Jesuit, Maurice de la Taille, has written a great work on the subject of the eucharistic sacrifice. Some Anglicans have followed his line of thought, notably Will Spens in his essay on the subject in *Essays Catholic and Critical*. The heart of Père de la Taille's theory is that there are several distinct parts in the single act of sacrifice. One is the actual immolation, or the slaying of the victim if that be the kind of sacrifice in mind; another is the ritual oblation or declaration of the meaning, intention, purpose, and value of the immolation; a third is the divine acceptance of the sacrificial act. Hence, it is claimed, the death of Christ on the Cross is the immolation; but the scene in the Upper Room, at the Last Supper, is the declaration of the intention of the immolation. The first element, the immolation, cannot be repeated; the second, the oblation or declaration, can be repeated. Indeed, the declaration or oblation must be repeated if the value of the sacrifice is to be appropriated. But because of the unity of the two elements, which can be distinguished only for purposes of classification and study, the truth is that when the oblation is made before God, the immolation, while not repeated, is present in and with the repeated statement of the intention of the action.

A valuable insight appears to be behind Père de la Taille's learned and interesting discussion. There is much to be said for it. But in criticism we must point out that the

French writer does not take sufficient account of the Church that offers the Eucharist. The Church, we believe, is the Body of Christ—and this in no vague sense but in the most real and vital sense, as our opening chapter sought to show. Since this is true, the eucharistic action must be much more closely related to the persisting identity of the Church than it is in the theory of Père de la Taille. In his view we find, so it seems, an almost mechanical relation between the events in the Upper Room and on Calvary, on the one hand, and the continuing Eucharist in the Church, on the other. This sort of thinking has always marked a certain strand in Roman theology, and from it our author appears not entirely to have escaped. He has done well, however, in showing that the eucharistic action is the way by which the historical event in the distant past becomes a living reality in the immediate present. This is the heart and center of the Eucharist. It is surely essential to insist that the carrying agent of the eternal and once-for-all sacrifice on Calvary must be the Body of Christ—which is to say, it must be Christ himself in his Church-Body who by his own action makes the 'memorial' of his 'death and sacrifice' an enacted and vitalizing reality. In this way the conception of the *anamnesis*, to which we have made frequent reference, may be usefully and rightly employed in the theology of the Christian Sacrifice.

We shall discover, as we proceed, that it is impossible to isolate the three notes that we have emphasized in our discussion of the Eucharist. In this, which is a memorial action, or an *anamnesis*, there is sacrifice, communion, and presence. Any one of these three without the others is bound to lead to an imperfect, truncated, and even untrue idea of the significance of the chief act of Christian worship. Christ is present that he may offer himself to God and so establish a communion between God and those who are members of the Body of Christ himself. Alternatively, Christ pleads his sacrifice in the mystical humanity which is his Church, so that, being present with his members, he may bring them into fellowship with the Father. Or, finally, Christ establishes between God and men a communion in which they may know their redemption, and share in the presence of the God-Man by whom reconciliation is effected. In each instance the presupposition is the Church as the Body of Christ. And in each instance the sacrificial note is strongly in evidence. In a true sense it must be primary.

The intention behind Père de la Taille's work is commendable. It is his purpose to show that the insistence on the Eucharist as a sacrifice does not have as its necessary concomitant the thought that Calvary is incomplete, that there is anything to be added to Christ's sacrifice, or that there is a repetition of the sacrifice once for all made in history. These are points we, too, are anxious to maintain. But the best way to do this, we believe, is by an adequate grasp of the nature of the Church as the Body of Christ, on the one hand; and by a proper understanding of the meaning of the 'memorial' or *anamnesis*, on the other. In fact, we believe this is the only way it is possible to maintain the points on which Père de la Taille would insist, while at the same time recognizing that the Eucharist as a whole is indeed sacrificial in nature.

As soon as the nature of the Church is correctly

understood, with a recognition of the deeper sense in which
'memorial' is used to describe the eucharistic action, it is
possible to see how that which was once for all done in
history may still be a present reality in the life of the
Christian community. For the Church of God is both *in*
and *inclusive of* the historic process. It is *in* the process,
since it is a body of men who become members of the Body
of Christ. It is *inclusive of* the process, since it partakes of
the eternal nature of Christ himself, whose Body it is, and
whose life permeates it and gives it his own vitality and
meaning. The Church, then, is double in nature, but not
merely because it has its divine and its human side. As a
corollary of this twofold nature, it is also eternal and
temporal, sharing in that simultaneity which pertains to
the divine element as well as in that successiveness which
pertains to the human element in its total life.

Here is the clue to the nature of the Christian Sacrifice. It is historic, in that it is concerned with the event
that occurred on Calvary for the redemption of the world.
This is the 'one oblation of himself, once offered.' But it is
also supra-historic, in that in 'commemorating' this event,
it partakes of that simultaneity which belongs to God himself, in the person of the Incarnate Lord. As the Body of
Christ, it shares in this inclusion of all time in its life. It is
not simply *of this present moment*, because to it *all* moments are present. Thus Calvary is both historic fact and
immediate reality, apprehensible when the actions of Christ
himself are re-presented by Christ in his mystical Body as
once they were performed by Christ in his physical body in
the days of his flesh.

The Eucharist might be compared to an optical instrument that focuses some scene and makes it available to the apprehension of the observer. Or it might be compared to a glass that gathers the rays of the sun and makes them a potent factor in a given situation and with a given context here and now. The sun is there as an established fact; the focusing is the means whereby that which is established fact is made present experience. So in the Eucharist, the action the Church performs is the way in which the benefits of Christ, and the redemptive work that made those benefits a possibility and a reality, are brought into the immediacy of the here and now, in the present and contemporary life of the fellowship, for those who are the members of the Body of Christ at this particular juncture. And by their participating in this action, the members of the Body of Christ offer their true and proper sacrifice, the sacrifice of Christ himself, with which they are united, and in and by which alone they are able to offer themselves to God the Father.)

It may be said, in criticism of this line of thought, that the approach is far too 'mystical.' This charge is based on a misunderstanding. Some theologians seem to entertain the idea that so soon as the statement of an important aspect of Christian faith is more imaginative and suggestive than logically exact, it is thereby either true only in a vaguely symbolic fashion or else a dishonest evasion of the difficulties that inevitably attach to simplicity and directness. But this is obviously absurd. The truths of the Christian religion, in any event, are far too profound ever to be fully comprehended by man; all the theologies of the

Church have ended in mystery, with a frank admission that they are but hints thrown out at great things that are beyond the grasp of the human mind. This does not mean that we are not obliged to seek such clarity as we are able to achieve, but it does indicate that we shall do well to keep a due humility in our statements. And it indicates also that theological statements, even at their best, are so limited by the finitude of the human mind that they can be no more than intimations, ideally true and sound, but never in the nature of the case utterly clear and mathematically precise. Even St. Thomas Aquinas was emphatic on this matter, and he is by all counts the most logical and rational theologian in the history of traditional Catholic Christianity.

The Christian Sacrifice is no exception to this general rule. The facts of the Church's life and experience are plain. The historic events from which the Church took its rise are equally plain, although there is sometimes less certainty about particular details than we might desire. The process of Christian development has taken a straight line from those events to those facts of life and experience. Christian theology is the attempt to construct some satisfactory statement, some articulation and definition, of this wonderful complex fact. But the rule is *lex orandi lex credendi*. Nowhere is this so obvious as in the Eucharist. That which is the rule of the life in worship is to be the rule of the interpretation of the rite.

But there is something more to be said. As we have pointed out, the Christian Eucharist comes to us as a development from the Upper Room; the Last Supper is the germinal fact. So we have historical data as well as experiential material which must be worked into whatever theological scheme we shall find possible. The whole complex fact is *confessional*, in that it is in and of the Church as the Body of Christ. With this in mind, we can see that the supposedly 'mystical' statement of the meaning of the Eucharist as a sacrifice is in effect nothing other than the attempt to state, in as direct language as is possible to us, but always with the admitted understanding that the language is at best imaginative and suggestive, the meaning of an experience that springs from the historic facts, is validated by centuries of practicing Christians, and is part of the total life of the confessional community which is the Body of Christ.

We might indeed add that there are two difficulties which are actually forms of one theological error, found in the extreme Protestant and in the Roman views of the Eucharist. In the former, the sacrifice in the Eucharist is rejected because it cannot be neatly reconciled with certain theological ideas. In the latter, the sacrifice is stated in language that often seems so definite and precise that it is impossible to accept it. Both are forms of the same fundamental fallacy—the notion that perfectly explicit statements can be made in an entirely logical manner about the subject. We believe that it is much wiser to approach the matter in the imaginative and suggestive fashion which we have indicated. Here there is room for mystery, but here, also, the reality of the Eucharist as a present fact of Christian life is plain, with all of its rich implications and its wide range of meaning.

Here, too, theology can be used to illuminate and

vivify the contemporary experience of the believer as well
as the historical faith of the Church. The Eucharist is much
more than a bare commemoration of the event in the Upper
Room without any reference to Calvary itself. It is not
related to Calvary simply by bringing into the mind of the
worshipper a devout attitude toward Christ's death. In the
Church's liturgy 'commemoration' is used in the true sense.
'Memorial' passes over into *anamnesis*. The redemptive
work of Christ is not finished long ago and therefore to be
accepted as a *fait accompli;* rather it is believed to be a
reality that can be entered into as living and immediately
available, present when the Church 're-calls' that which
Christ did. Here the sacrifice of Christ is made into a fact
that has once been accomplished but that is also accomplished again and again as the believers are enabled (in
communion and fellowship with God through the reconciliation made on Calvary) to dwell in Christ as he dwells
in them.

When the central relationship between the Christian Sacrifice and Calvary has been established, there are
even wider ranges of meaning. Christ, in reconciling *men*
to God, reconciles *the whole created order* to God. The
Church, as Christ's Body, appropriately offers to God, in
the eucharistic action, the life of all its members, including
their work and play as well as their religious life. It offers
to God the homes and shops and farms and offices and mills
in which his people work. It offers to him the natural world,
with its resources and its produce. Indeed, it offers to God,
in and by and with the sacrifice of the death of Christ here
pleaded, the entire created order that Christ came to re-

deem. There is little need to dwell on this point because the writer has discussed it at some length in a small book entitled *The Divine Action*, and there is an excellent study of the subject in A. G. Hebert's *Liturgy and Society*, where the wider implications of the eucharistic sacrifice are mentioned. The whole 'liturgical movement' of the present day has been toward bringing these truths before the eyes of the worshipping Christian, thereby redeeming the Christian's Sacrifice from any suggestion of 'religiosity' or of parochial narrowness.

As Christ offered himself by the Holy Spirit to the Father—here the Epistle to the Hebrews once again is helpful—so the Church's sacrificial action and the participation of the faithful are by the work of the Holy Spirit. For that Spirit is the Responsive Person in the Blessed Trinity. He it is by whom all things return to their Creator; he it is who is the great 'Amen' in the world of history and nature, as well in the inner life of the Godhead itself. The eucharistic action of the Church is not independently accomplished; it is performed by the Spirit, who in and through the Body of Christ conforms men to Christ himself. Thus the ancient maxim, that the worship of the Church is offered to the Father through the Son's mediation and by the instrumentality of the Holy Spirit, is vindicated as being an exact description of the eucharistic sacrifice. The ancient liturgies largely demonstrate this. The Eastern Orthodox insistence on the necessity for the invocation of the Holy Spirit, although inadequate as a theory of consecration, is a way of emphasizing the reality of the work of the Spirit in the eucharistic action; while some of the Anglican Books of

Common Prayer, with their reference to the Spirit's work in the sacrament, are more explicit than most of the other Western liturgies.

⌞ In this respect, as in so many others, the Eucharist reproduces in microcosm that which macrosmically is true of the whole divine operation. The sacrament in which, as Aquinas says, 'our whole salvation is comprehended,' succinctly sums up and by its action presents theological truth. While it is only by Christ's sacrifice that we may 'make bold' to claim God as our Father, it is only by the Spirit's indwelling action that our pleading of Calvary can be effectual. Because the eucharistic offering is blessed and sanctified by the Holy Spirit in the Church, it may be made to God 'in remembrance of [Christ's] death and passion,' so that those who are 'partakers of his most blessed body and blood' may by that double reality of sacrifice and communion become 'one body with him, that he may dwell in us and we in him.' ⌝

The trinitarian content of the Eucharist, therefore, is an important element in the action. It might be said that the Eucharist is best interpreted as the sacrificial offering of the life of the Church—which is Christ and his members, Christ in his members, and Christ with his members— to the Eternal Father by the Eternal Son in and by and with his continuing incarnate Body the Church, in the power of the Holy Spirit. In this light the sense in which the Eucharist is truly the Christian Sacrifice becomes quite clear once more. This is the manifest intention of that section of the Prayer Book liturgy in which the pleading of the sacrifice of Christ and the offering of 'our selves, our souls and bodies, to be a reasonable, holy and living sacrifice,' are linked together and, as it were, identified. In the Eucharist, 'the passion of Christ which is our sacrifice' is pleaded and offered by the Church to God the Father, not as a new thing but as that eternal yet historic reality by which any and every approach to God must be made. This is the true sacrifice; this is that rite which men have always been seeking. If it be proper to say, with Father Tyrrell, that there is only one religion underlying all the 'religions'—one religion which is man's search for God in response to God's everlasting search for man—it is also proper to say that the history of religion, in the sense of sacrificial offering and worship to God, is all of a piece. And if Father Tyrrell was right in adding that this 'one religion' finds its culmination and end—in von Hügel's grand phrase, 'its implied goal and center'—in Jesus Christ in the Catholic Church; so it is also right to say that all sacrificial worship finds *its* culmination and end, *its* implied goal and center, in the Christian Sacrifice, where the Incarnate Word in his Body the Church offers himself to the Father through the Holy Ghost.

6] *The Eucharist as Communion*

'The cup of blessing which we bless, is it not the communion of the blood of Christ? The Bread which we break, is it not the communion of the body of Christ?'

In these words, St. Paul has given classic expression to the fact of Christian experience that is established by participation in the Eucharist. Here the faithful are brought into a fellowship with their Lord that is deeper and more real than any other possible for men. It is a fellowship in which he is one with them, and they with him, so that it can be described only in terms of mutual indwelling; the Anglican liturgy says that we are 'made one body with him, that he may dwell in us, and we in him.' The table discourse at the Last Supper, as the author of St. John's gospel portrays it, is in this vein; and it is for this reason, among others, that we should regard that gospel as a transcript of early Christian experience, even if it is not a veridical account of the details of Christ's life and words.

The attempt to achieve communion with deity through participation in a sacrificial meal is not uncommon in the religions of the world. Like sacrifice itself, it has a certain universal quality and appeal, expressing some deep need and desire of the human soul. Robertson-Smith, in his work on *The Religion of the Semites*, sought to show that this conception was behind the Jewish sacrificial system;

whether or not his contention can still be sustained in detail, it is surely true that there is an important and significant value in it. And it can unquestionably be maintained that classic Christianity has interpreted the Christian Sacrifice in this fashion—as an offering to God in which by participation the worshipper shares, thereby entering into communion with the object of his worship.

The Episcopal Church, with other denominations, so frequently uses the term, 'Holy Communion,' as a description of the Eucharist that there is never any question concerning this particular aspect of the sacrament. Indeed, it may be suggested that the constant use of the term has been the cause of a considerable misunderstanding of the actual nature of the Eucharist among church people. They tend to forget or overlook the order of significance that the Prayer Book Catechism, for example, suggests when it puts *first* the fact that the sacrament was instituted for 'the continual remembrance of the sacrifice of the death of Christ,' and *some time after* speaks of it as food for 'the strengthening and refreshing of our souls.' The same misunderstanding is responsible for the prevalent and sentimental practice of Maundy Thursday evening 'communion services,' in memory of the Last Supper. The objection to these services is that the Eucharist is simply not, in intention or significance, a memorial of the Last Supper. [It is, as we have seen, a memorial or *anamnesis* of Calvary, or Good Friday, and what was there accomplished for the salvation of men.] The Eucharist is no sentimental love feast, nor is it an instance of happy table fellowship. By the act of our Lord himself at the Last Supper, it became something else—

it was turned from a meal of religious fellowship into the remembrance of the redemptive work of Christ. The communion that is established is a communion established in that redemptive work, and it is a communion in 'the benefits which we receive thereby.' If the defenders of the Maundy Thursday evening observance were familiar with their catechisms, they would not be likely to commit so egregious and silly an error as that to which their weakened and sentimentalized theology leads them.

On the other hand, the infrequency of communions that was for many years so noticeable in the Roman Church, and which Pius X and now the liturgical movement have been seeking to correct, represented an equally serious departure from the true meaning of the Eucharist. [Without the opportunity for a general communion of the faithful, the significance of the sacrament is dangerously perverted. The easy excuse that at least someone makes his communion—namely, the celebrant—is no excuse at all; the point is that the incorporation of the faithful, by communion, into the Body of Christ in vital fashion, whereby they realize their true character as baptized members of that Body, is so essential to the eucharistic idea that without it the expressive act of Christian worship becomes seriously defective.] This does not mean that there may not be occasional services when the number of communicants is limited; nor does it make it impossible for a Christian to attend the celebration now and again, as may be convenient, without communicating. It does mean that the normal rule of worship should be the offering of the Eucharist as the great sacrificial action of the Church, with a general communion of

the people in which they share in the life of Christ, returned to them as the holy gift of God to his holy people.
When this norm is observed, sacerdotalism will never appear; the Catholic doctrine of the priesthood of the laity in
the Body of Christ will be maintained; Christ, who is the
common Life of the members of that Body, will be the
center of Christian devotion.

The fact that the Eucharist is regarded by Catholic
Christianity as the chief means of fellowship with Christ,
and with God in Christ, indicates at once that historical
Christianity is not an ethereally 'spiritual' religion. It finds
its best avenue to life in God by way of material things,
broken and blessed in a sacrificial context. To this sacramental insistence in Christianity, which is part of the genius
of the religion of the Incarnation, we shall give special attention in the next chapter, where we shall discuss the presence of Christ in the Eucharist. But it is important here to
see that the normal communion of the Christian with God,
as the Catholic centuries have understood it, is through a
sacrificial sacramental rite, rather than by personal, private
devotion. The latter is not underestimated or rejected; it is
set in its correct context and related to the corporate action
of the whole body of the faithful. For Christianity is a corporate religion, in which men find new personal lives in a
fellowship with God that is enjoyed not in isolation from
but in solidarity with their human brethren in the mystical
Body of Christ himself. This is indeed the specific quality
of Christianity, as distinguished from those religions that
may, perhaps rightly, be characterized in A. N. Whitehead's famous aphorism, 'what a man does with his solitari-

ness.' That comment could never define Christianity. In our religion there is certainly an insistence on relationship with God, but it is always found as part of the total picture of the ransomed community, the 'blessed company of all faithful people,' in which by Christ—and more particularly by participation in the Christian Sacrifice—the believers are made 'very members incorporate' in a living fellowship.

Communion with God for the Christian, then, is no 'flight of the alone to the Alone.' Neither is it unmediated communion with God. It is in terms of Christ and through him. This is true both with reference to the peculiarly Christian fellowship with the Father and also with reference to all fellowship with God, wherever enjoyed. Christ is by definition the Eternal Word of God, the 'measure of the unmeasured Father,' in St. Irenaeus's phrase; and 'no man cometh unto the Father but by' him. It is through the Eternal Word, 'by whom all things are made' and who is 'the light that lighteneth every man,' that all knowledge of God and *all* communion with him is effected. The Word is divine—'of the same substance as the Father'; yet he is the outward-moving, expressive Action of God—'God from God.' For the specific Christian communion with God, the same principle holds good, but here it is the *incarnate* Word by whom God and men are brought into communion. Furthermore, it is the Incarnate Lord in his Body the Church who mediates between God and men. It is right, therefore, to see that the kind of relationship with the divine reality sustained in Christianity is established in and given by the unique action in which the divine-human Jesus is 'remembered' in his redemptive work. This work, as the Epistle to the Hebrews says, is the 'new and living' way to the Father; it is through the 'veil'—that is to say 'the flesh' of Christ—through his sacred humanity and that which was done by him in that humanity, now shared by those who partake of his humanity in the Church and are members of his Body and recipients of his life.

      If the incarnate action of God is the means for Christian, as distinct from general, communion with God, then surely the crucial moment in that incarnate action, the focal act that is the 'one oblation of himself once offered' on Calvary, is the peculiarly effective moment in which God and man are brought together. Calvary is not separate from the rest of the incarnate action; it is the summing-up and the making-clear of the whole of it, in a vivid and compelling fashion. So when we speak of the communion of the Christian with God effected in the Memorial of the Passion, we are not forgetting all that Christ did and does apart from his redemptive work in its specific sense. Yet it is the specific redemptive act that gives a unique quality to everything else; it is appropriate, therefore, to see that the Eucharist is the way in which 'God and man are reconciled.' To repeat a statement made earlier, the notions of Incarnation and Atonement are so intermingled in Christianity, or rather are so identified, and the relation of this twofold fact of Incarnation and Atonement to the Church's eucharistic action is so definite, that the Christmas sermon by Becket in T. S. Eliot's *Murder in the Cathedral* is singularly apposite —at the *Christmas* Eucharist, the Archbishop preaches on the *Passion of Christ*.

      It is in terms of Christ, through Christ and in Christ,

that the Christian has his fellowship with God. And it is specifically in the sacrificial action of Christ on Calvary that this reconciliation is established and the fellowship between God and man made truly possible, in the freest and fullest sense. Thus it is appropriate and indeed inevitable that the Christian Sacrifice is the occasion of man's meeting God— meeting him in the divinity that is united with manhood in the God-Man. But this is not all. [For communion in Christ with our brethren of the human race is also given here. This at once brings us to the difference between *camaraderie* or merely human fellowship, so treasured by us all, and the quality of communion with our brethren that is available for the Christian.] Failure to make this distinction has given rise to all sorts of errors, not least to that which teaches that the principal purpose of Christianity is simply to bring men together in brotherhood. To unite men is both commendable and desirable, not to say utterly necessary, if human affairs are to be carried on with anything like decency, in peace and concord. But that is not *Christian* fellowship.

Christian fellowship, or communion with our brothers in Christ, is a *crucial* matter, in the literal sense of the word. William Langland's words about Calvary,

> Blood brothers we became there,
> And gentlemen each one,

express the fact of Christian fellowship. Because men find themselves at one in the humanity that was shared with them by God in Christ, and in finding themselves so united are brought together in the depths of their being, they are truly and utterly brought into the enduring brotherhood that is in Christ. This brotherhood is based on a participation in the facts of suffering and death; it is vindicated in the Easter triumph of Christ; and it is a victory over the sin and frustration that beset the human race.

In other words, the peculiar quality of Christian fellowship is that it is not something which man *achieves* but something which God *gives in Christ*. Hence it is something into which men enter; it is an already present reality, now shared by those who become one with incarnate God. This is the meaning of the seventeenth chapter of St. John's Gospel, to which reference has already been made: 'That they all may be one, as thou, Father, art in me, and I in thee, that they also may be one in us . . . I in them, and thou in me, that they may be made perfect in one . . . that the love wherewith thou hast loved me may be in them, and I in them.'

In one sense, of course, such unity is given in membership in the Body of Christ: that, in truth, is the significance of baptismal regeneration. In another and deeper sense, the unity is given in the Eucharist, since here the Church *does* what it is: it makes into a common brotherhood in Christ those who have been made brothers in him. Such is the thought behind St. Augustine's wonderful phrases in which he speaks of the Church as offering what it is when it offers the Eucharist; or again, when he says that in the Eucharist the Church receives what it is. Once more we see that the central conviction of the Church as the Body of Christ is involved here as in all other areas of eucharistic theology.

St. Paul, whose words about communion we cited at the beginning of the chapter, has the same thought in mind, for he goes on in the verse immediately following to say, 'For we being many are one bread, and one body; for we all are partakers of that one bread.' It is in the eucharistic action that the unity of man with man in Christ is established and given, as it is also in that action that communion with God in Christ is made available and actualized for us.

The communion of the Christian in the Eucharist is with God and with man, because it is communion in 'the body and blood of Christ,' who himself is God and man. It is also communion with the entire creation, both above man and below man. The creation *above* man is included, for man is united 'with angels and archangels, and with all the company of heaven,' in lauding and praising God; the communion of saints is not a vague dream but a realized fact when the Eucharist is offered. The creation *below* man is included, as well, since the material elements that are used have been taken into the sphere of the eucharistic action, given their proper employment in the scheme of things, and related as they should be to God and his will: 'the whole earth is full of thy glory.'

But central to this, not contradicting it but confirming it, is the Cross of Christ. That is the point of reference; it is the pledge and the promise that broken things, frustrated things, sinful things, may be restored and in Christ are restored to their God-intended purpose. Even man, with his wilful defiance of the divine intention, is restored to his true and proper place. Here is the rightful ordering that is the foretaste of heaven, the perfected communion in and with God, who is 'all and in all.' Hence the communion breaks through death and includes those who have departed this life, the holy souls who are reaching toward God and the saints who are with him forever. Communion could go no further, for it includes the entire hierarchy of being, from God himself down to the lowest level of created matter.]

This, again, is the reason it is right to say, with Mr. Eliot in *Four Quartets*, that despite its tragic side 'yet we call this Friday *good*.' The sacrifice of Calvary, shared in and pleaded by the Body of Christ, is not tragedy, although to worldly eyes it may seem so; it is victory beyond all understanding, for 'God is reigning from the Tree.' The communion of the believer with God and man is one that is given at this deepest level. Hence it is all-inclusive; it is a sharing in that which is ultimately good and of *the* Good, which is God triumphant and glorious.

The thought of the worshipper must never be centered exclusively on Calvary, to the loss of the victory that Easter and the Ascension signify. The life that is shared is the life that 'was dead and is alive again.' The risen Lord still bears 'those dear tokens of his Passion'; but he is the risen Lord, and the communion with God and man is communion in the risen life of the crucified Christ. The Eastern Orthodox Church has expressed this aspect of the Eucharist much more directly and consistently than the Western Church. We of the West have tended to give our attention almost entirely to the sacrificial action in the Eucharist. It is right to attend to this. But it is not right to do this if we overlook the truth that the sacrificial action both in itself and in its result is a *victorious* action. On the other hand, our brethren in the Orthodox Communions have perhaps erred in failing to place sufficient emphasis on the sacrifice —although it is admittedly difficult to appraise Eastern spirituality, and in any case the total effect of the Eastern liturgy would seem to give balance to the eucharistic action.

The communion with the divine Reality that is enjoyed by the member of the mystical Body of Christ is different in quality from other relationships with God; the communion with his fellowmen is likewise different from ordinary human brotherhood as 'the world' understands it. Our intention here is not to cast aspersions on natural and general communion with God and with men, relationships common to the human race and to all religions and moralities. The Christian does not consider these evil; he regards them as imperfect. They are good in their way, and in their goodness are preserved and sanctified in the new Christian relationship effected in Holy Communion. Nor are the ties of nation and family and home evil; they require for their perfection, however, to be taken into the life that is found in Christ. There all natural bonds receive a new and wonderful significance. This is the reason the nuptial mass is celebrated at the marriage ceremony; a natural relationship is by this means made more than a communion of persons, becoming a communion of man and wife in Christ— which is a very different thing.

The communion with God enjoyed by non-Christians is likewise not denied or rejected in the insistence that Christians know a different quality in their communion with

God in Christ. The 'unincarnate' Word (in von Hügel's phrase) has never left himself without witness among his human creatures, and it is the glory of our race that all men have the capacity both for some knowledge of God and for some experience of his presence in their communion. Yet the Christian, whose communion with God is in Christ the incarnate Word, knows the fulfilling of these adumbrations and intimations, in company with his fellow believers and as member of the very Body of the Word himself. It is this, too, that is the crown of man's possibility as man.

The communion with God in Christ, which is shared in the life of the Church and made a living reality in the offering of the Christian Sacrifice for those who assist at this expressive action of the Body, is a new level of being, a new emergent, in the order of things. It is that new level in which the *historic* fact of God in human life, the Lord Jesus Christ, is made a *continuing* fact in human experience. The Christian is thereby a man of the *type* Christ; he has a share in a higher order of reality, the order of God-manhood, or human life in God. The Johannine literature is filled with this sort of teaching. The communion into which we enter in the Eucharist is a communion in which we are raised above the level of human life as otherwise known, and are introduced into an experience that is an earnest of heaven. The eschatalogical element, therefore, is an essential part of the Christian's worship. When St. Paul says that 'ye do shew forth the Lord's death, till he come,' he is stating in his own idiom the fundamental, more-than-this-world aspect of the Christian Eucharist. The action is a first sign—a true but, as it were, introductory share—of the kingdom of heaven.

We have seen that at the Last Supper our Lord intended to make the disciples sharers in the life that would be brought about through his sacrifice. They were proleptically enjoying the Kingdom which was not yet come. The Eucharist still has this meaning. The fullness of man's destiny is neither achieved nor achievable in space and time; the Kingdom is still to come. But the first fruits, the earnest, of it are here and now, as the eucharistic action takes the worshipper, with his brethren, into heaven itself and there brings him into communion with God in that full and free fashion which is to be the life of the Kingdom. Because this is true, the same full and free communion is established between man and man; while the whole created order plays its part in the final fruition which by its earnest is already present and given. The Christian Eucharist takes in the full sweep of Christian faith, and is meant to lead into a life in grace which will reflect that faith and be properly empowered by communion in the sacrifice.

Throughout the present discussion, we have spoken of the life in Christ which is given to the communicant. In our next chapter we shall treat in detail the problem of the nature of the presence of Christ in the Lord's Supper. We must not anticipate that question, but we must here indicate something of the quality of life which is involved in such communion as we have described. The life that is shared in this sacrament must be definable, although of course not with the precision of mathematical or logical propositions.

In fact the new life in Christ, which is the basic

reality of the communion in the Christian Sacrifice, is adequately suggested in the single word, 'charity.' This word has had many and varied meanings, but fundamentally and in the New Testament sense it is twofold in significance. It means an outward-moving awareness of others, with a sensitivity to their personalities or selves. It is not sheer kindness, but it includes that; neither is it sentimentality, although it may certainly involve a right sentiment. Perhaps the best single synonym is the Quaker word, 'concern.' For the members of the Society of Friends, 'to have a concern' means to be sensitively aware of another person, of his situation and his problems; it means entering as deeply as possible into his life and sharing with him, so far as can be, the particular cares which are his. To have charity, in this sense, is to share in the life of God himself, for 'God is love'—*agapè*, which is precisely this word charity. Similarly, it is to be related to one's fellows in such a way that there can be the completest give-and-take in a thoroughly unself-centered life—unself-centered because the center of life is God, and everything else and everyone else is seen and known and loved in and for God.

St. Paul is correct, in his great list in Philippians, in setting down 'love' as the first of the fruits of the Spirit, to be followed by 'joy, peace, long-suffering, kindness, meekness, self-control.' It is this quality of life that is shared in communion with Christ. This is God's life, as it is mediated to us through the divine humanity and as it is adapted to our human situation. Among the fruits, and crowning them all, is charity. But charity is to be linked with faith, by which the apprehension of God is made possible, and with hope, which is life toward God in the attitude of 'tip-toe expectancy,' as Baron von Hügel delightfully phrased it.

The wording found in the Pauline reference raises another important point. He speaks of 'the fruit of the Spirit'; and this implies that the quality of communion as found in the Christian Eucharist is in some way related to the Holy Spirit. Precisely so. For the Church is marked by the 'fellowship—or communion—of the Holy Spirit,' a phrase that really means 'the fellowship in Holy Spirit'; and, as we have seen, the Spirit is the effectual agent in the whole eucharistic action. As believers are caught up in that movement which is the work of the Third Person of the Trinity, they come to share in the life of the Second Person, and are united in love with the First Person. 'The grace of our Lord Jesus Christ, and the love of God, and the fellowship of the Holy Ghost'—this puts it succinctly and satisfactorily.

The communion which the worshipper has with God and man in the eucharistic action may vary in intensity and in degree of conscious realization from time to time and from occasion to occasion. It is psychologically unlikely and pragmatically impossible to think that every time the Christian assists at the sacrifice he will have an equally strong and vivid apprehension of that which is taking place. Indeed, it is quite possible that the more frequently and regularly the communicant fulfils his duty in this connection, the less strongly he will feel the experience itself. But this is not to be wondered at. It is not only a matter of psychological law; it is also a matter of theological principle. An unsound, though popular, view these days is that the work of God upon us is determined by the degree of our

awareness of it. To say it is so determined is to overlook
the vast area of the subconscious and unconscious mind,
and the tremendous influence of the impressions made upon
us in ordinary experience by things of which we are not
vividly aware. Furthermore, it is to identify God, at least
in this regard, with a 'state of mind,' or at any rate to suggest that his operation may be so described. The cult of
'religious experience' in the narrower sense has tended to
be dangerous, because it has introduced to certain minds a
whole series of difficulties that in truth are nonexistent.

'God is greater than our minds'; he is also, as Canon
Oliver C. Quick is said to have remarked, 'greater than our
feelings.' It may well be that we are close to Christ, in intimate communion with him, at moments when the sharp
awareness of this communion is absent from us. Yet this is
not unlike some quite common human experiences. One is
often most intimately in fellowship with some loved friend,
with one's wife or with one's children, at moments when
there is no keen and psychologically vivid awareness of that
fact. There may be nothing much to show for it, excepting
that 'it is good for us to be here.' We find a certain sustained and sustaining satisfaction and joy, even if the mo-
mentary experience is itself unexciting, in the fact that we
are together with those we love. It is not otherwise with
the communion that the worshipper may have with his
Lord, and in that Lord with the divine Reality and with his
fellowmen.

The only requirement made of a communicant is
that he shall be one who is in faith and penitence. That is
to say, he shall believe that God will do again that which

he has always done in this sacrifice; and the communicant shall try, so far as it is possible for him, to be in a state wherein he may receive God's gift. If these two conditions are fulfilled, he is delivered from further worry; it is then in God's hands to grant what he has promised, in whatever way he may see fit. God can be trusted to do what is best for each one of us, because he knows us as we are at each particular time and in each given circumstance. That is all; and that is enough.

It was suggested in the last chapter that the elements of sacrifice and communion were closely associated in the Eucharist; this chapter has perhaps done something to justify that assertion. But it was also maintained that these two are linked with the presence of Christ in the eucharistic action, since without some genuine sense in which Jesus Christ, 'God and man, body and soul' is truly present in, with, through, by, and under the bread and wine which are 'eaten and received' by the faithful, the meaning of the sacrifice and the communion will be lost. For Catholic Christianity in all its forms, what has been termed 'the real presence' is indispensable. If that reality is denied or minimized in such a way that it becomes simply a 'figure,' the historic meaning of the central rite of Christian worship is gone. This eucharistic action is a rich complex; hence we must make room for all the strands that have gone into it, both historically and in the experience of the Body of Christ. We now consider the Eucharist as the presence of Christ. The conviction that he is present there, and that being present he is to be worshipped, is (as von Hügel used to insist) 'the heart of Catholic devotion.'

7] *The Eucharist as Presence*

Of the importance of one fact in Western religious history there can be no doubt whatsoever. The very controversies about it are in themselves an indication of its importance. [This is the belief that in the Christian Eucharist, the Lord Jesus Christ is truly present, in substance and in very self; this has been for Catholic Christianity the heart of religious experience.] Departures from that conviction by sectarian groups have been part and parcel of an unbalanced theological pattern, if the faith of the early centuries of the Church is to be taken as the criterion of religious proportion.

Eucharistic adoration, directed toward Jesus believed to be present in the consecrated species of bread and wine, has reached extraordinary heights in the Western Church, with types of devotional practice that are quite unknown among the Eastern Orthodox. The Western mind, especially in its Latin and Anglo-Saxon representatives, wants a concrete focusing of its object of worship. Perhaps this is part of that temper which has made it possible for science to develop in the Western world; whereas the Eastern world, in its primary concern for the universal and eternal issues, has not been so fruitful in science. In any case, the truth is that the Western Church has very definitely made its whole religious life center in Christ really present in the Eucharist. The Church has tended to look with suspicion on mystics who thought or claimed that they might have some direct, unmediated, non-sacramental way of approach to their Lord. On the other hand, such notable mystics as St. John of the Cross, St. Theresa of Avila, and St. Catherine of Siena were markedly institutionalized and sacramental souls.

In her book, *Worship*, Miss Evelyn Underhill erroneously assumed and argued that the Englishman is by nature not inclined to eucharistic adoration in anything like the degree to which this is true of other Westerners. The fact is that much of the highest development of eucharistic devotion came from England, as has recently been conclusively demonstrated by Dom Gregory Dix in his little pamphlet, *The Detection of Aumbries*. It depends, indeed, upon whether one is singling out certain English religious writers, like Walter Hilton, charming and profound as he is, or whether one is concerned with the generality of English devotion as seen in the popular piety that brought about in England the strong eucharistic life that was best expressed in processions of the sacrament, extraliturgical devotion before the reserved sacrament, and the like. We are not now interested in defending any or all of these practices, some of which seem to be right, and others of which we may consider inordinate—in the sense that they involve exaggeration of a correct theological position by a potentially dangerous devotional practice. What we are attempting to show is the inaccuracy of the assertion that Englishmen—and thereby, it is assumed, the Anglican Communion in all its branches—are not as likely as 'romantic' Latin peoples to center their worship in the Eucharist, and especially in the Lord Jesus believed to be present in that action.

It is true that the Anglican Communion has been unwilling to indulge in precise definitions of the *how* of the presence in the Eucharist. It is also true that there has been in Anglican writing a wide variety of eucharistic theories, varying from the sympathy for receptionism that Richard Hooker in certain of his moods seems to express, to the assertion of a presence in the elements of bread and wine, which Hooker also appears to make on other occasions, and which has in fact been the more consistently Anglican position. But neither of these negates the Anglican Church's intention that the Eucharist shall be the chief service each Sunday, as is shown by its direction that at this service alone sermon, announcements, and alms are mentioned; nor do these truths deny the teaching that the Eucharist is a sacrificial action in which all the worshippers are to share. Above all, they do not for one moment destroy the total impression that the Anglican liturgies without exception give to the non-Anglican visitor: that the eucharistic bread and wine are more than mere symbols or figures, in our modern sense of these words—that they are the 'body of our Lord Jesus Christ, which was given for thee' and the 'blood of our Lord Jesus Christ, which was shed for thee.' The words of the Prayer of Humble Access state this as a matter of sheer fact: 'Grant us, therefore, gracious Lord, so to eat the flesh of thy dear Son Jesus Christ, and to drink his blood, that our sinful bodies may be made clean by his body, and our souls washed through his most precious blood . . .' No other known liturgy is stronger than this in its assertion of the reality of Christ's presence, or in its identification of that presence with the bread and wine of the eucharistic sacrifice.

Historically, there have been several theories concerning the manner of this presence. The Roman Church has officially set its stamp of approval upon Transubstantiation, in which it is said that the substance or underlying realities of the bread and wine are changed into the substances or underlying realities of the body and blood of Christ, while the accidents or external signs remain bread and wine. This view depends upon the scholastic philosophy developed chiefly by St. Thomas Aquinas. For those who can accept this philosophy, it is cogent and perhaps convincing. Nevertheless, the charge, made in the Anglican Articles of Religion, that it 'overthroweth the nature of a sacrament' is, we venture to think, correct. For if the definition of a sacrament is, as von Hügel expressed it, 'one thing working in and through another'—or, in the Prayer Book catechism's phrase, 'the outward and visible sign of an inward and spiritual grace' (we should prefer to say, 'inward and spiritual reality')—then Transubstantiation certainly is false to sacramentalism, because it suggests, indeed insists, that bread and wine must in some fashion lose their proper identity in order to become the vehicle for the spiritual reality of Christ. It is as if one said of the Incarnate Lord that in order to be God-Man, he must not be genuinely and really man in the center of his humanity; his rational nature must be transformed into the eternal Word, or that Word must take the place of his rational nature. The former of these theories is the Eutychian heresy, the latter the Apollinarian heresy; and it seems that, *mutatis mutandis*, the doctrine of Transubstantiation is the eucharistic counterpart of one or other of these.

We shall see, however, that the insight on which this view rests is central to Christian devotion. The conviction of the Catholic Christian is that the Lord Jesus so uses and operates in and through the bread and wine, so thoroughly makes them the instrumental vehicle of his presence, that they are relatively insignificant, as bread and wine, in the thought and adoration of the believer. This is a *spiritual* or *religious* conviction. But it is dangerous to construct a metaphysical theory such as Transubstantiation on that basis alone, until one has considered all other aspects of the question, especially the nature of sacraments as such. One thing we must say in favor of Transubstantiation, however, is that it is a highly 'spiritual,' and in no sense a gross or carnal, view of the presence of Christ. The frequent misunderstanding of the doctrine found among ignorant or ill-informed folk does not for a moment mean that the theory itself is less than 'spiritual'; the discussion by St. Thomas in the *Summa* makes this entirely clear.

The Lutheran equivalent of Transubstantiation is Consubstantiation. In the strictly Lutheran theology, Luther's peculiar view of the ubiquity of Christ's humanity is involved. But if this particular notion is dismissed, the theory of Consubstantiation becomes an assertion that while the substances or inner realities of bread and wine remain, there are *added* to them the new substances of the body and blood of Christ. Luther maintained this view with vigor. Because other Reformers tended to minimize the reality of the presence in such a *substantial* sense he declined to co-operate with them in certain regards—his controversy over *Hoc est corpus meum* bears this out. There is a danger that the theory of Consubstantiation, if pressed, may lead to a notion of the eucharistic presence that is the counterpart not of the Apollinarian heresy in Christology, as is the case with Transubstantiation, but of the Nestorian error. In the heresy condemned under that name, it was held that the divine and the human in Christ were, so to say, loosely united, held together by what was on the divine side 'good pleasure' and on the human side 'obedient will.' *Mutatis mutandis*, the eucharistic doctrine taught, as Consubstantiation might suggest, that the body and blood of Christ are indeed related to the reality of the bread and wine, but not in any essential fashion.

Two other theories may be mentioned briefly. One is 'classical' Virtualism, the belief that the *virtus*, the grace or strength of Christ, is imparted through the eucharistic elements; but no affirmations are made concerning substantial identity. The other is 'classical' Receptionism, which is the view that the presence of Christ is in the believer as he receives the elements, but not in the elements themselves. Neither of these theories will receive further attention here, since both of them fail to certify the eucharistic presence that we have seen to be part of the eucharistic *idea* of the historic Church. The truths that each maintains—and which each erects into a self-sufficient theory of the sacrament—are adequately preserved in the central eucharistic theology, but in that theology are balanced by other and more central ideas. In our discussion of the subject, these truths will play their part in the total picture. This must be our apology for an apparently cavalier dismissal of the two theories. The same charge might perhaps be made about our brief comments on the opposite theories, Transubstantiation and Consubstantiation. The proper emphases in the several views can readily be preserved in a theory of the manner of the presence, which is more in accord with a general sacramental theology and in agreement with the doctrine of the Incarnation as classically defined at Chalcedon.

One important comment must be made here, however. This concerns the term 'real presence.' There are two meanings of this phrase. The first is that the presence of Christ is a real one—in the sense that it is a *genuine* presence. Such an assertion is made over against a merely figurative presence of Christ in the Eucharist; and it would probably be made by all Christians, from Zwinglians to Catholics. For each and every one of them, Christ is really present in the sacrament. The problem is *where* he is present and *how* he is present. The second meaning of 'real presence' bears on this latter problem. For it states a *praesentia rei*, a presence of the *thing itself*—which means in this case a presence of Christ in his proper reality, body and soul, God and man. There may be, and we shall indeed find that there is, need to show that the terms in this connection are to be taken more in the religious than in the logical sense. But to speak of the *res* of the sacrament, a usage followed only in regard to the Eucharist, is to speak of the presence of the underlying reality of Christ, present not by his influence or grace or benefit, but in *himself*. Our intention in this discussion is to defend and expound the 'real presence' of

Christ in the bread and wine of the Christian Sacrifice, in both senses of the phrase.

The essential truth that the doctrine of the 'real presence' seeks to preserve is that Jesus Christ, in the total integrity of his person as God-Man, is truly present as the *res* of the sacrament, to be received in Holy Communion. Furthermore, he is truly present as the *res* of the sacrament also, to be pleaded in sacrifice:

> And having with us him who pleads above,
> We here present, we here spread forth to thee . . .

He is truly present as the *res* of the sacrament in such wise that, being present there, he is rightly to be worshipped. *He* is to be worshipped; it is not the sacramental elements in their *natural* order that are adored, although by reason of their direct association with him they are to be reverenced and treated with utmost care. No Catholic theologian of any school has ever maintained that the natural elements are the object of worship; it is always Jesus Christ sacramentally present in those elements for the 'strengthening and refreshing' of the faithful who is 'to be worshipped and adored.'

This is indicated by the insistence of St. Thomas Aquinas, repeated in another connection by Cardinal Newman, that when the Blessed Sacrament is carried from one place to another, Jesus Christ himself is not carried. For the reality of Christ is eternal and simultaneous, and can never be moved by human agency from place to place since he is present in all space and all time. The point of the eucharistic presence is that he is especially present, in a mode especially adapted for human reception as the heavenly food of the faithful. In St. Thomas's classic phrase, this is a presence of the body of Christ, but not a bodily presence.

It is necessary to make these remarks because the *cultus* that has developed in connection with the eucharistic elements has frequently been the occasion for serious misunderstanding by those who have failed to acquaint themselves with the true meaning of belief in the presence. No one of the devotions in question is directed toward the bread and wine on the altar or in the tabernacle or aumbry. In each case, the adoration is *through* these to the hidden presence: *Adoro te devote latens Deitas:* 'Humbly I adore thee, Deity unseen.' Or, as in the great prayer of St. Thomas Aquinas, who is the doctor *par excellence* of eucharistic piety, we ask that we may 'at length with unveiled face contemplate forever' him 'whom we purpose to receive *veiled*' in the Christian Sacrifice during this our earthly pilgrimage. There is no doubt that some of the Roman Catholic extravagances in eucharistic devotion have tended to suggest what might be called, not unfairly, a 'christianized baalism,' in which to all intents and purposes the sacred host is regarded as divine. But it is not right, or charitable, to judge a devotion by the abuses to which it is liable, or to reject it because it has sometimes been improperly indulged.

In the Eucharist the theological problem is to maintain the distinction that in sound religious practice is made between the true reality of Christ spiritually present in bread and wine, and the physical elements themselves, while insuring that the religious intuition so ineptly stated in Transubstantiation is also maintained—the intuition that since Jesus Christ *is* here present, his presence is the governing and controlling factor in the situation, rightfully receiving the adoration of the faithful. The problem is precisely the same as that which theology handles in the doctrine of the person of our Lord himself. In Christology it is necessary to distinguish between the Godhead and the manhood of the Incarnate One, while at the same time recognizing that the *theologically* false monophysite heresy is, *religiously* speaking, only an inaccurate statement of the profound intuition that all devout Christians have—that in Jesus Christ the devotionally dominant and, as it were, 'engineering' reality is the Godhead who is to be worshipped.

First of all, then, what is meant when one speaks of the body and blood of Jesus Christ as the *res* of the sacrament? Traditionally, this has been taken to mean that the bread is spiritually identified, in some true fashion, with the body of Christ, while the wine is similarly identified with his blood. That which is present under the species of bread is the body of Christ, that which is present under the wine is his blood. But there is a serious problem here, upon which the later theory of concomitance has its bearing. This theory, now standard doctrine with the Western Church, maintains that the *whole* Christ is received under *either* species, so that the communicant who takes only the wafer receives the 'body and blood' of Christ; and similarly with the chalice. It has sometimes been said that the doctrine of concomitance is simply an attempt theologically to justify a modification of liturgical practice in the Roman Church—the withholding of the cup from the laity. To some extent this is doubtless true, as a matter of historical development.

But we believe that the development itself has behind it a profound truth that is relevant at this point.

If the 'whole Christ' is given and received—and therefore is to be adored—under either species, it is plain that the terms 'body' and 'blood' are being used in a somewhat different sense from that in which they are conventionally employed. St. Paul is authority for the assertion that 'flesh and blood cannot inherit the kingdom of heaven'; by this he implied, certainly, that physical terms cannot properly be used to describe spiritual realities, if the former are taken as being exact definitions. On the other hand, they can and must be used, analogously, if we are to speak of spiritual matters at all. The difficulty is that far too often it is assumed that predication in these realms must be either strictly univocal (with one meaning applied to the terms in both levels) or equivocal (with a total difference in meaning given the terms). The truth is that the use of any and all terms taken from the physical or material realm and applied to the spiritual realm must be analogous: that is, there must be sufficient identity of meaning to make the use of the terms intelligent and intelligible, but the identity must be consistent with a vast difference in the implications and suggestions of the terms in the two areas of discourse.

If the risen Lord Jesus Christ does not possess 'flesh and blood' in any *physical* sense—and this must surely be true—the only way these terms could be applied would be by analogy. That for which 'flesh' and 'blood,' or 'body' and 'blood,' *stand*, that which they mean and signify in our human understanding of the level of physical and material things, that they also stand for and signify when they are applied to the spiritual realm, but with the qualification that the signification differs according to the realm under discussion. When we say that we shall have 'spiritual bodies' in the resurrection, we are neither identifying the bodies so described with our present physical bodies nor implying that bodies in the resurrection will be exactly like our physical bodies. On the other hand, we are not saying that there is no connection whatsoever between the two. We are affirming that what our bodies stand for here and now will be sustained in some spiritual fashion in the resurrection. Our bodies stand for our total personal identity, our continuing selfhood, all that we have known and experienced in the here-and-now; they are our vehicles for self-expression in the temporal sphere. Our 'spiritual bodies,' then, will be the continuing medium for our self-expression, maintaining our total personal identity and selfhood through and beyond the dissolution of the physical. This is *religious* idiom, but without it we should tend to become all too spiritual in our thinking; and if we pressed the literal univocal signification, we should reduce our experience to the purely physical level.

Perhaps this illustration will help us in our attempt to discover the meaning of the terms 'body' and 'blood' as applied to Christ's real presence in the Eucharist. 'The whole Christ' is present and given. The terms 'body' and 'blood' that are applied, aptly enough and following our Lord's own usage at the Last Supper, are appropriate for the truth that his risen humanity, which does not possess 'flesh and blood' in the physical sense but is human nature in its true and eternal reality as God understands it to be, is conveyed to the faithful under the forms of bread and wine. Yet there is none of that corporeal and carnal identification which might be suggested if the terms were taken entirely literally. The 'body and blood of Christ' in the Eucharist stands for the real humanity of the risen Lord, continuous with and identical with the humanity which is his from the Blessed Mother, which suffered on the Cross, and which rose triumphantly on Easter Day. It does not mean body and blood in a physical sense; it means body and blood in the sense they have for God—the vehicle of an offered Life that is expressed, as by an instrument, in a 'bodily' fashion.

The use of these terms prevents any gnostic evaporation of Christianity into a religion of ethereal and unreal spirituality. Some clergymen, disliking to use the word 'blood,' have substituted such a word as 'love.' Here we have gnosticism rampant. It is not the 'love' of Christ that is communicated to the faithful, although that surely is a consequence of their humble reception of the sacrament. The true humanity of Christ, in its integrity, is communicated. And where that humanity is communicated, the deity that by the Incarnation has been hypostatically united with it is also communicated. So it is indeed 'the whole Christ' who is given, 'God and man, body and soul,' in von Hügel's phrase; the presence is *totus Christus*, not an ethical quality or a spiritual influence.

It has often been pointed out that the 'body' is the effective instrument of self-expression; that indeed is its metaphysical signification. And to the ancient Jewish people, blood meant 'life offered to the point of death.'

These two facts are pertinent. The risen humanity of Christ is his self-expressive instrument. Life, true manhood, expressed in human flesh and blood during the days of Christ in Palestine, is the same life, true manhood, that is expressed in risen humanity or 'spiritual flesh and blood.' The very concreteness of the terms is their peculiar value. Aldous Huxley, in a different connection, has remarked that 'there is one thing about a body: it is indubitably *there*.' There is one thing about the humanity of Christ present in the Eucharist: it is indubitably *there*. Similarly with the blood of Christ. There can be no evasion of the reality of the living manhood of Christ in the Eucharist when such a term as 'blood' is applied to it. This is life in no ultra-refined, docetic fashion; it is true life, once lived after our own earthly fashion and now after a heavenly manner, but the same persisting life, expressing the same one Christ our Lord.

The real trouble is that it is hard for some people to recognize that language is used in different senses for different purposes and in different kinds of discourse. Professor Theodore Meyer Greene, of Yale University, makes a helpful suggestion on this subject. He notes that the language employed in science is of one type, that employed in conceptual or philosophical thinking is of another, and that employed in æsthetics is of a third. Then he argues, valuably and persuasively, that while the language used in religious discourse is sometimes of a conceptual type, as when philosophical discussion concerning religious beliefs is undertaken, it is more natural both in worship and in much dogmatic definition to employ the kind of language that is appropriate to drama and even to poetry. Professor Greene carefully points out that this does not for a moment imply that the language so employed is 'untrue.' It means simply that this method of stating truth is appropriate to the particular area of reality that is under consideration. Unfortunately, many people have the notion that poetry is something that is 'not true.' The actual fact, says Greene, is that poetry, or at least poetic language, *is* true; but it is of a different order of truth from humdrum matter-of-fact 'truth,' which indeed is frequently so partial and abstract that it is hardly true at all, excepting for quite limited and specialized purposes.

If this theory of the use of language be allowed, we have still another reason for insisting that the terms 'body' and 'blood' are to be taken very seriously indeed in our discussion of the Eucharist. But they are not to be taken *literally*, if by that we mean in a physical and material sense. In fact, Professor Greene's view is entirely in accord with our present treatment. In particular, his insistence on the genuine and essential truth-value of terms that are applied in imaginative fashion would seem to serve our purpose admirably. One hopes that other writers will follow his line of thought, thereby helping us to see that the 'intentionality' behind the Church's constant claim that we must speak of the 'body and blood' of Christ in the Eucharist has its foundation in a fact of such supreme importance that, so far as the Christian Sacrifice is concerned, all Christian faith and experience depend upon it. For surely the conviction that the Eucharist is a sacrificial action, in which a true communion with Christ (and thereby with God and man united in him) is made possible, requires that the real humanity of Jesus, now risen and triumphant, as well as his eternal Godhead, are both of them present in, with, through, and under the species of bread and wine.

We turn to a discussion of the manner of the eucharistic presence, especially in its relation to the elements of bread and wine. That Christ is present, and that the presence is directly related to the elements, is not for us a matter for question; we assume that this is part of the essential eucharistic *idea* to which we have so frequently referred. Any theory of the mode which we may offer will necessarily be tentative and by way of suggestion; we do not hope to offer a final and exhaustive explanation. The mode of the presence, in relation to the elements, will always be a mystery. The human mind is not able to comprehend more than dimly the way in which God can use this or any other means for effecting his purpose and conveying his presence.

The best starting place for an understanding is surely the Incarnation itself. It is to be remembered that the accepted dogmatic definition of the person of Christ includes several terms: his Godhead, his manhood, their union in Christ. The *Godhead* in the Incarnation is not altered, modified, or limited in any fashion by the act of God in becoming man; orthodox theology declares that God the Son, without essential change in his nature or attributes, took to himself human nature, in all its essentials. God remains God, then, without modification. But man also remains man. Doubtless the *manhood* of Jesus is unique in that it represents in its origin a greater degree of divine initiating activity than there has been in any other instance: this is the theological significance of the doctrine of the Virgin Birth, much more important than the biological aspect of the doctrine. But with this exception, the manhood of Jesus is manhood in the usual sense of the term. The fact that it is manhood without sin does not contradict this statement, for manhood with sin is to that degree less than true manhood. Sin is a disease, not an inevitable concomitant of humanity, despite the fact that all men excepting Christ partake of the 'sin of Adam' by virtue of their human solidarity. Christ is the intimate and direct *union* of Godhead and manhood in such a way that here, in this single instance, humanity is taken up into its right and proper ordering, and is used, without essential change, although with supremacy and excellence in degree, for the purpose of God's self-expression through his Eternal Word. As St. Athanasius put it, the human nature born of the Virgin Mary is the *organon* or instrument for God the Word in his specialized and concentrated action.

In the Eucharist, bread and wine, good realities in the order of natural creation, are in similar fashion taken by God and made to serve the purposes for which God intends them: that is, to be the *organon* or instrumental vehicle by which the humanity of Christ, risen and triumphant, is made present and available to his members in the Church. The analogy to the Incarnation is clear. Our Lord's risen humanity remains as it always is, that medium in which God through his Word, among many other things that the Word does, specially and, so to say, directly acts upon men. The bread and the wine remain bread and wine, but are now put into the new sphere of operation that God has established for them; they serve, in St. Augustine's words, as *signa sacra,* by which the presence of Christ is made possible in his humanity as holy food for men's nourishment. The union of bread and wine with the risen humanity of Christ is the *new* reality, specifically: only here and in this connection do bread and wine have this particular use. Once they have been so used, it may be recognized that all common meals, and all food received together, have a certain capacity for conveying intimations of the presence of God, but they cannot convey the risen humanity of Christ in the eucharistic sense; only the Christian Sacrifice can do this.

The implication of the theory of Transubstantiation, according to which bread and wine no longer remain bread and wine but possess only their 'accidents' or outward and visible *appearances,* is not required in our view; hence 'the nature of a sacrament' is not overthrown. But the fact that the bread and the wine now have their primary significance as the *organon* for the risen humanity of Christ safeguards the intuition behind Transubstantiation. The reality of Christ in the sacrament is so strongly the 'prior' truth that for purposes of devotion it chiefly matters. Yet it is not that *alone* which matters. What is central is that the God-Man is in continued, direct, and intimate relationship with mankind through the eucharistic presence, in a way that is even more peculiarly humble and wonderful than the fact of the Incarnation itself, for here it is the Lord Jesus working through simple creatures of human sustenance. But if Transubstantiation is ruled out, the possible implication of Consubstantiation, which is the suggestion of an incidental and accidental relationship of the two substances or inner realities, is also avoided, since it is maintained that the bread and wine are directly and (as it were) necessarily used by the risen humanity of Christ as the instruments of his sacramental presence.

This reality that is given to the Eucharistic elements by consecration is not brought about by any human action. It is brought about by our Lord himself, when as Head of the Church which is his Body he desires to make himself continually available to his members. The prayer of the Church, uttered by a priest and ratified by the faithful, is the petition that God may do this thing: the result of the prayer is the divine action and the divine action only. No one 'makes God': God gives himself—or rather, the Lord Jesus Christ gives his humanity under bread and wine, and with his humanity gives his whole person, since he is eternally the undivided, unchanged, unconfused, and inseparable union of Godhead and manhood.

The view we are advocating might be called divine instrumentality or instrumentalism. It involves the belief that God *is* where he *acts*, but that his actions involve not presence as at a distance, but presence in immediate reality. The bread and the wine are taken into the sphere of the divine operation in such a fashion that they serve purposes not habitually predicable of bread and wine. They possess in this context capacities that bread and wine do not commonly possess; they provide in this context what Dr. Spens has called 'opportunities of experience' of another sort than those usually offered by bread and wine. And the change is by the divine will, not by human contriving. This view requires a strong conception of the Church as the Body of Christ, for the Church *is* the new context. The action of the Church in offering the Eucharist is not the action of a group of religiously minded men who would know Jesus; it is the action of Christ in his Body, making himself known to those who are his members by baptism. Aquinas, in his eucharistic prayer, part of which we have already quoted, says: 'Grant me so to receive the Body of thy only-begotten Son, our Lord Jesus Christ, which he took of the Virgin Mary, that having been incorporated into his mystical Body, I may ever be accounted among his members.' It is our Lord's intention that his members be so strengthened as worthily and rightly to fulfil their membership in him; the holy mysteries of his Body and Blood are the way in which he has chosen to do this.

The fact that by consecration the bread and wine become the instrument for the presence of the risen humanity of Christ is a fact that, once accomplished, does not pass away. Some writers who have followed a line of thought not far different from that advocated in this chapter have said that the presence of Christ vouchsafed in the elements is for the space of the immediate eucharistic action only, and is withdrawn as soon as that action is completed. But this is to overlook the truth that the eucharistic action, as we have seen, is not merely temporal action: it is an action that has an eternal side. The presence that has been given is a persisting presence. The bread and wine are not removed from their place in the new sphere of the divine operation, since that operation is not completed until the elements have been received by the faithful 'to their soul's health'. Hence, the eucharistic elements, after the particular moment of the sacrifice is completed, temporally speaking, remain the instrumental means for the true presence of the risen humanity of the Saviour. Dr. Spens has dealt faithfully with this question, making clear that the presence rests not upon human but upon divine intention, and insisting that the reality given to the elements by consecration is dependent not on our human movement but on the risen Christ's desire to be with his people.

For this reason, the reservation of one or both of the consecrated species for the purpose of communion by those who are ill, or who for some other valid reason are unable to take part in the offering of the sacrifice, is right and reasonable. More than this, the direction of devotion, either privately or in regulated public worship, to the person, of Christ, present in his risen humanity through these instruments, is right and proper. For where Christ is, there he is to be worshipped and adored. Hence the practice of prayers before the reserved sacrament has nothing perverse about it; danger could arise only when such prayers take the place of the total eucharistic action, making it seem a needless addition to, or an optional part of, the worshipper's life. Certainly Christ is present in any church building —and everywhere else, for that matter—by virtue of being what he is. But he is present in a particular mode in the eucharistic species; and when he is so present, he is to be given the worship that belongs to him as Head of the Church and Lord of our lives.

The possibility of danger in so-called extra-liturgical

devotion is illustrated by the way in which popular Roman Catholic piety has frequently tended to become more addicted to such services as Benediction and the Forty Hours Devotion than to find its right center in the liturgical action itself. Certain types of people will always be attracted to these special services. It is far from our intention to condemn outright this kind of devotion. But it has a tendency to supplant the Eucharist in the popular mind, and emphasizes so exclusively only one of the essential aspects of the Eucharist that it is to be regarded with some suspicion. In this sort of piety we find little or nothing of sacrificial offering by the Body of Christ. An imperfect idea of the meaning of communion is suggested with passive adoration of the Lord Jesus in the Blessed Sacrament quite excluding everything else in the Eucharist as it has come to us historically.

Occasional services of eucharistic adoration, such as might be held on Maundy Thursday night (instead of the unfortunate and more frequent 'Memorial Service of Holy Communion') and on other feasts like *Corpus Christi*, are both fitting and proper; they do not tend to overthrow the balance of eucharistic piety. Here, as in so many instances, it is not the thing itself that is wrong, but its inordinate use. The intention ought always to be such a proportionate and proper emphasis on all parts of the Christian Sacrifice as shall bring before the worshipper the gospel and shall help him to participate in the offering of the sacrifice, in the adoration of the truly present Lord, and in a communion with his Master that shall end by making him worthy 'to be accounted among his members.'

This brings us to the conclusion of our treatment of the three interrelated aspects of the Eucharist. It is a Memorial Action, in which the Sacrifice of Calvary is pleaded and entrance into it made possible; in which members of Christ are at one with their Lord and hence with God and their brothers in the Body of Christ; and in which Christ himself is present to be loved and worshipped. Since this is true, the manner of observance of the Eucharist is a matter of no slight importance. The setting of the Eucharist, its ceremonial accompaniments, the ritual that is employed, the whole atmosphere of the action, are vitally significant.

8] *The Celebration of the Eucharist*

All of us are familiar with the complaint that the manner in which the Christian Eucharist is celebrated in what are frequently called 'the liturgical churches' is very different from the Supper in the Upper Room, in which the Eucharist finds its origin. As a matter of fact, no one has ever denied that there is a difference. But it is only in comparatively recent years, and among those who tend on the whole to take a low view of the sacrament and to deny that it is the essential and characteristic expression of Christianity, that this difference has been used as a criticism of the manner of eucharistic celebration in Christian communions of the Orthodox and Catholic traditions. Previously, this difference has meant nothing more than the obvious truth that a deepening understanding of the significance of the Eucharist has inevitably led to such ordering, regularizing, beautifying, and dignifying as shall plainly manifest the central place this action holds in the life of the Church itself.

No one in his right mind would think that the process of development in this direction has been only a matter of aesthetics. The results may be, and indeed are, strikingly beautiful and appealing to the aesthetic sense, but it is not beauty alone that is intended. Nor would anyone with common sense think that wicked ecclesiastical minds have been at work here, complicating things for the sake of greater enhancement of the priestly office. The truth is that we tend always to dignify what we esteem highly; what is done frequently and consistently, we tend to regularize and formalize. Above all, in what is done with group participation as one of its primary features, we conform to given patterns or series of patterns that can be followed with relative ease by those who take part in them. These are the considerations that should be in our minds when we note the way in which the Eucharist has developed from the simple meal in the Upper Room, through the more or less informal gatherings of the primitive period, into the well-ordered Eucharist of the early Church, and finally into the pattern that has now become familiar to us, whether in its Eastern or in its Western manifestation.

In a previous chapter, we spoke of the series of 'sub-actions' that necessarily occur within the total action of the liturgy—the offering, the blessing, the fraction, and the communion. These are *constants* in all parts of Catholic Christendom and may be taken for granted. So may the fact that the developed Eucharist has attached to itself, the liturgy of the Word of God, with readings from the Scriptures and a sermon or exhortation. With this we are here not concerned. Our interest is in the total setting and ceremonial accompaniment of the sacrament, rather than the particular form of words or arrangements of the several details in the ritual—for ritual means, of course, the words used, and not the actions performed, despite a prevalent misunderstanding of the term during the past hundred years.

The setting of the Christian Sacrifice is that of 'external religion,' in Father Tyrrell's phrase. The term *external religion* describes the fact that by things which are
done with the body and to the senses, spiritual transactions
of supreme importance are carried on. This is a point of
view that is opposed to the etherealism we mentioned
earlier; it is an insistence that the body, quite as much as
the spirit of man, has its part in the worship of God and
in our religion. The whole setting of the eucharistic action
of the Church is an assertion of the reality of external religion, its importance and even its necessity in the life of the
believer. Since the peculiar quality of man is that he is 'an
animal substance with a rational nature'—which is to say,
mind-body and body-mind—and that he can never be properly understood excepting as one who dwells in the two
realms of sense and of spirit, the external side of the Eucharist has its own peculiar significance. It is worship adapted
to the nature of man, as he is actually found, and not as
some might wish him to be; man is not a disembodied
spirit, he is no angel—pure spirit without body—and he can
never be treated as if he were.

But the fact that the setting of the Eucharist is external religion is also a consequence of the sense of the
action itself. For the primary definition of a sacrament is
that it is an instance of a spiritual reality operative in and
through a material or visible or tangible reality; the outward
and visible is as essential to the totality as is the inward and
spiritual. The nature of a sacrament requires a setting in
which due regard is had for the external. Nor is this a contradiction of Christian truth, since the focal belief of his-

toric Christianity is the Incarnation, in which the supreme spiritual Reality is declared to have taken to himself human nature, which includes a material and physical body. The whole picture hangs together. The Incarnation, the sacrament, the nature of man, the external religion employed in the sacrament—all are of a piece.

The one requirement of external religion is that it shall be consistent with the spiritual truth that is involved, that it shall be free from all suggestion of magic or superstition, and that it shall be morally in accord with the high standard set by the faith. There must be no degrading of the religion as a whole by the introduction of practices that are immoral or intentionally superstitious—this is the kind of evil that illustrates the truth of the old saying, *corruptio optimi pessima*. To use the whole man, body included, is desirable in religious practice; to spoil such use by unethical or magical excesses or abuses is to do almost irreparable harm. Hence it is necessary constantly to check and correct popular devotion, which sometimes may get out of hand and go beyond the limits of the faith. For this reason the words of the liturgy are prescribed and have the authoritative sanction of the Church, through its theological doctors and its saints, who guard it from the danger of exploitation by the exaggeration, the perversion, and the emotionalism of some one man or some group of men. The mind of the Church is our trustworthy guide in keeping sanity and healthiness of spirit in the celebration of the Eucharist.

The Christian Church's Sacrifice is a *social* action. The context of the Eucharist is the life of the mystical Body of Christ, and there can be no valid—that is, rightly authenticated—sacrament apart from that Body. We are not here entering into the so-called Cyprianic-Augustinian dispute on the nature of the Church, which arose in relation to the *traditores*. We need only remark that even if St. Augustine was right in affirming that sacraments outside the Church, performed by properly ordained ministers, are valid, he was saying this simply as a means of affirming the Church's charity in refusing to confine God's grace. He was not denying the essential nature of 'Church connection' which would indeed be involved by the fact that the schismatic ministers had been properly ordained according to the intention of the Church, although in these instances without its specific approval or sanction. The sacraments belong *in* and, in one sense, *to* the Church; by that token they are social expressions of the Church's life. For this reason we are bound to realize that an ecclesiastical ordering of the Christian Sacrifice is inevitable. The *whole* group must take part in this cult action; the members of the Body of Christ must not be left to the vagaries of individual ministers, or for particular congregations to set themselves up as independent judges or private practitioners of that which belongs to the *whole* Body. The eucharistic *idea* demands that the offering of the Christian Sacrifice shall be for and by and in the Church as the Body of Christ, with every member able to assist as a functioning agent. The practical consequence is such a formal setting for the Eucharist as shall make for easy and intelligent assistance.

Whatever may be said on behalf of the use of languages partly or totally unknown to the worshippers—and probably there is something to be said for this, or else it would not have been so prevalent a practice—the real danger is that it makes right participation in the service almost an impossibility. 'A language understanded of the people,' in the phrase from the Anglican Prayer Book, seems required if there is to be that 'reasonable, holy, and living' action in which all the people have their part and place. That this position is correct is demonstrated today by the fact that the best minds in the Roman Catholic Church are trying to have parts or all of the Roman liturgy in the vernacular, thus coming round at this late date to the principle that the Anglican Reformers enunciated and put into effect in the sixteenth century. The *kind* of vernacular to be employed is another question, of course. Vulgarity, cheapness, the merely contemporaneous idiom have no place in the worship of God, publicly conducted, as the Memorial of the Passion of Christ. The vernacular should be the *best* language of the time, with only such archaisms as are meaningful to the congregation, but with the dignity and sobriety of the native tongue in its highest reaches of dignity and aspiration. All who belong to the Anglican Communion may be glad that we have this sort of liturgical expression in the Book of Common Prayer, although there are not a few places where meaningless archaisms could be changed into proper contemporary phrasing without ruining the dignity and style of the book.

We mentioned just now the 'style' of the liturgy. The whole question of style or character of expression is highly important. As the characteristic action of the Christian Church, the Eucharist must reflect and convey the life in faith that marks the Body of Christ; it must also effectively represent the great dogmatic affirmations by which that life is made a possibility and an actuality.) The notes we may single out as requisite in the liturgical expression of the Church's life and faith are four: *dignity* (or *order*), *mystery, humility, confidence*. To each of these we shall give brief attention, without suggesting that there are no others which might have been selected, and without assuming that the particular order in which we have chosen to list them is in itself necessary and logically exact. But it is apparent that these four are found in the celebration of the Christian Sacrifice by the great historic communions.

The *dignity* or *order* of liturgical expression in the Christian Sacrifice is a reflection of the balanced and proportionate life and the right ordering of the faith that belong to the Christian Church. The way in which this is manifested in the celebration of the Eucharist is primarily in the regular, calm, unhurried yet expeditious performance of their proper parts by the several sacred ministers, including the celebrant, the assistants in the sanctuary, and the congregation, which itself is ministering in being present to fulfil its proper liturgical function of offering the Passion of Christ. The fact that the words are prescribed delivers the faithful from the vagaries of individual priests; the ceremonial gestures and movements are dictated by tradition, so that they too have acquired a certain formalization or 'style,' which prevents idiosyncrasies that distract the attention and disturb the worshippers. To use a phrase employed in a very different connection by the English critic, Clive Bell, the eucharistic action has taken on a 'significant form.' By this we mean that the large element of stylizing, prescribed action and prescribed speaking has acquired a significance or intentionality that is so integrated by this time into the whole service that something of importance is lacking when the form is not followed.

All of us have attended services in which failure to follow the usual form has disturbed our own devotion and has made it difficult to participate fully in the offering of the Memorial of Christ's redemptive work. Surely the responsibility of a priest is to reduce his own individuality in the Eucharist in order to make possible the fullest congregational participation consistent with the rite. Yet he must make sure that the meaning suggested in the words and actions does not become utterly lost in what is as bad as over-individualism—a purely automatic performance of the liturgy, in which the man becomes a machine and not the functional person for the Body of Christ. When the Eucharist is celebrated with the dignity of great drama, but without any attempt at artificiality, it reproduces with astonishing directness the Christian tradition, taking all our senses and using them for the glory of God, and in intimate relation to the redemption that is being celebrated.

Bodily movement, for instance, is part of the eucharistic action. The elements must be handled, the bread broken, and the chalice taken. But when due regard is had for the full faith in the Eucharist and its high significance, this minimum is greatly expanded. Bowing and kneeling, the brief act of adoration known as genuflection, beating the breast in token of unworthiness, even walking from place to place with erect posture, not to speak of simple gestures such as opening and raising the hands in invitations to prayer, have their contribution to make to the dignity of the whole. The honor accorded to the gospel book, and the procession associated with it; the preparation of the offertory, with the assistance of servers and the use of vessels specially designed for this purpose; the ceremonial washing of hands: these are some of the countless small details that give to the Christian service of worship a deepened meaning attaching to physical and material things, and bring about an ordering and dignifying of all that is brought into the sanctuary. The congregation, likewise, has its part to play. Standing and kneeling, gestures such as the sign of the Cross, and numerous other familiar ways of behaving have their contribution to make to the total action. Singing, chanting, the use of rich and varied colors, and the ancient practice of burning incense are not to be forgotten. The variety that these provide, as well as the changes in vestments, hangings, and music that mark the seasons of the year, has perhaps more to contribute than any other element in aiding the faithful to grasp and appreciate the balance of the Christian faith.

The dignity of the celebration of the Eucharist is one of its most important aspects, conveying the sense of a tradition into which the worshipper enters, and in which he finds an already present faith suggested and given. The dignity of the rite is one element in the *givenness* of the Christian religion; it is not something newly invented or discovered, but has about it the richness that comes from ancient use.

The second of the notes about which we are speaking may be conveniently termed *mystery*. The Christian faith itself is a mystery, in that it is an intimation and hint of truths that are never comprehended fully by the human mind, but must at best be apprehended suggestively and imaginatively. The Eucharist, too, is a mystery—a partial intimation, in outward form, of a truth that is inward and hidden. So it is right that in the celebration of the Christian Sacrifice, the element of the *mysterium* should be found. Otto in his *Idea of the Holy* has tried to make this notion of the mystery, which attracts yet inspires awe, the peculiar differentia of religion. Probably he has erred, as so often happens, in overemphasizing an idea that is new to much modern religious writing. There are other aspects that must be taken into account in any adequate definition of religion. Yet the sense of mystery, which draws the worshipper and at the same time puts him in a state of 'religious fear,' is singularly important and cannot be underestimated.

Otto is correct in singling out the celebration of mass as one of the best examples of mystery in this religious sense. The whole service is built about ideas which in their fullness cannot be logically defined or rationally expressed. The presence, the sacrifice, the communion—here are facts beyond simple statement; they must be made manifest in an 'evocative' fashion. The Eucharist includes much that is allusive, much that awakens curiosity but leaves it not entirely satisfied, much that deepens awe and yet stimulates interest. The strange thing is that this was never the conscious intention in any part of the development of the service. It *grew* that way. The pieces, each one of which was quite different in origin, came together so that the result is an evoking of the numinous sense in man, answering to the *mysterium* suggested to him by 'what goes on.' He feels there is more there than can be put into words; there is more there, even, than meets the eye of the worshipper. Some great and transcendent action is in process: the worshipper participates in it and yet beholds it in wonder and adoration.

For Christian faith, this is of course true. What goes on in the Christian Sacrifice literally passes human understanding, since in it God is at work. Here the redemptive work of Christ is re-presented; here communion with the source of our being is mediated through Christ; here the very presence of God incarnate is found, in bread and wine that instrumentally render available for adoration and reception the risen humanity of the God-Man. This is quite obviously a mystery into which no man can hope to enter more than a few steps: 'Ye do shew forth the Lord's death till he come.' It is right that the atmosphere of the liturgical action should suggest the mystery, even though it does this without conscious intention and simply by reason of truth breaking through language and movement. Professor C. C. J. Webb has remarked that Christian doctrine is 'a hint thrown out at a great mystery'; in a similar fashion, the Eucharist is an intimation of a great mystery and itself partakes of that quality. This is an 'incomprehensible but indefinitely apprehensible' action.

Humility is the third note to which we call attention. The far too frequently criticized Prayer of Humble Access in the Anglican Prayer Book admirably expresses the humility that pervades the whole eucharistic action: 'We do not presume to come. . .' Or again, the words that

precede the eucharistic *Our Father* teach the same truth:
'. . . we are bold to say.' They both indicate the reverence
and lowliness of heart that must accompany any approach
to the God whom Christianity proclaims. Or once more:
'And although we are unworthy, through our manifold
sins, to offer unto thee. . .' The Anglican liturgy illustrates
what is true of all historic liturgies—they are permeated by
the spirit of humility, the quality of soul that is the human
pre-condition for any divine action upon man.

Lately some strong attacks have been made upon
this whole idea. We have been told that no Christian ought
to say that it is a 'bold' thing to approach God; we have
been informed that the Prayer of Humble Access is grovel-
ing in spirit. One can only suspect that the authors of these
criticisms have hardly considered the nature of the God
whom the Christian approaches, the nature of man as he
approaches God, and our entire dependence upon the person and work of Christ for any 'worthy access' to our
Creator. This is no sub-Christian cringing before a fierce
deity. It is the recognition of the facts of God's holiness,
righteousness, and awful love, on the one hand, and of our
own stained characters, imperfect lives, and unloving behavior on the other. As St. Anselm said, in his frequently
quoted comment, there are some 'who have not yet considered of how great a weight is sin.' It is our sinfulness as
well as our littleness that brings reverence and humility of
spirit into our attitude toward God.

The Christian life is a humble life. It is not humble in
the sense in which Uriah Heep was humble—that was a
sham. It is humble in the sense in which St. Francis of

Assisi was humble. With all the Poverello's trust in God as One who loved him, he was humility itself as he spent the nights in prayer. His Canticle is nothing but humble recognition of God's greatness, while he never forgets that he himself is one of God's creatures and hence related as creature to his Maker. Humility is in a way the sense of humor that recognizes oneself for what one is—a tiny creature against the vast purposes of God and the wonder of his universe; what is more, a sinful creature, who ventures in all his littleness to interpose his puny will between God and the accomplishment of God's great ends. The humble man is the man who knows the truth and accepts it, willingly, loyally, uncomplainingly: he is tiny and he is sinful, and there is no getting away from the fact.

Humility is the condition that precedes the saving action of God in Christ. If we are not in the way of accepting a gift, we shall never know Christ's redemption. Pride in human achievement, glorying in our own gifts or abilities, the kind of self-assurance which implies that we can save ourselves—all this is a sure way to render nugatory the salvation of Christ. It is a matter of faith and experience that the one soul into whom Christ's grace can find no entrance is the proud and self-sufficient soul; on the other hand, all faithful Christians know that as their soul humbles itself in the presence of God's gift, it becomes the recipient of grace beyond its farthest imagining.

The Eucharist expresses this. Its celebration is not marked by vulgar enthusiasm, by cheap exuberance. The offering of the Christian Sacrifice is reverently done, its liturgy filled with expressions of unworthiness; with kneeling, where it is indicated, to show that the humility is genuine; with contrition for sin; with acknowledgment of unworthiness; with humble acceptance of, and humble joy in, God's forgiveness. Dr. Howard Chandler Robbins has used the fine phrase, 'the solemn joy of plainchant,' to describe such Christian humility when it seeks to express its happiness in God's action. The plainchant, as he remarks, is the only fitting music to indicate this.

And yet humility in the Eucharist is mingled with another note, the last of our four. This is *confidence*. For if the Christian is humble in saying it, he is yet *bold to say*, 'Our Father.' He is certain of God's being, God's love, and God's care; he is assured of the salvation wrought by Christ; he knows himself to be a member of the Body of Christ, indwelt by the Holy Spirit; he is profoundly thankful for the surety of his trust that in the Holy Sacrifice he pleads Christ's death, knows his presence, and is in fellowship with him. All this may and must be held and believed with humility, as a great gift; it also may and must be held and believed with a sure confidence that gives life a splendid significance and a noble assurance. These two notes are found intermingled throughout Christian life and faith, for while the believer is humble, he is also sure. Like the New Testament writer, he can say, 'I *know* whom I have believed, and *am persuaded* that he will keep that which I have committed unto him.'

Confidence is found in the whole stately movement of the Christian Sacrifice. There is no hesitation, no delay; it moves on confidently, from the opening Collect to the high moment of sacrificial pleading, of eucharistic adoration, and of holy communion. God has made his promise; Christ is surely there; the sacrifice is truly commemorated; the fellowship with the Lord is certain to be consummated. It is because of the divine pledge that the human confidence can be so real. The eucharistic action is marked by humility, but in that humility it is sure of its purpose and of its fulfilment. The whole Church has learned this assurance, and each member of the Church may share in that which the Body of Christ knows, no matter how weak his own faith may be at any given moment. In the Eucharist the believer can rest back on the corporate confidence of the community, when his own lamp of conviction burns low. The formal quality of the service, its 'stylizing,' is a statement of the surety of Christian faith as the Body of Christ maintains it.

Here, then, we have a remarkable expression of Christianity in its liturgical action. The dignity, mystery, humility, and confidence that belong to the Christian tradition are vividly placarded before the eyes and almost unconsciously communicated to the soul of the believer. The Christian Sacrifice is centrally and essentially *Christian*, clearly and unmistakably a transcript of the faith and life that are known by that name. The soul 'formed' by the eucharistic action is bound to be a soul 'christianized' to the core. The inner life will be molded and shaped by the action of the liturgy, not merely because of what it is in itself but because of the setting it has created for itself and the atmosphere that it generates. Thus the Eucharist operates upon the believer to make him indeed an 'other Christ.' The kind of sanctity that eucharistic life establishes and creates is not that which is so often thought to be essentially Christian—the kind of busy-ness and moralism that is frequently confused with our religion. Rather, the Eucharist establishes and creates a kind of sanctity that is best described as 'life in Christ,' the awareness of the Supernatural and its ever-present pressure, of which 'good works' are but an overflow.

This type of piety, which is distinctively associated with the Catholic tradition, is nourished primarily by the participation of the faithful in the eucharistic action. Such participation is indeed essential to the Eucharist. The tendency in some areas of Western Christendom to make the offering of the Christian Sacrifice a purely sacerdotal function, at which the laity present do little more than 'hear mass,' has had a most unfortunate effect on the entire religious life of the Roman Communion. It has been part and parcel of that separation of the teaching and the learning Church, that gulf between the ministry and the whole Body of Christ, which in large measure was responsible for the abuses of the late Middle Ages and thereby precipitated the Reformation. It is a separation that has colored much of the thought and practice of European Catholicism since that day, and from which the contemporary liturgical revival in Rome is violently in reaction. Dom Gregory Dix, whom no one can suspect of anti-Romanism, has faithfully handled this particular subject in his book *The Shape of the Liturgy* and also, more directly, in his essay in *The Parish Communion*. One of the unfortunate accompaniments of the Catholic revival in the Anglican Communion has been the way in which the degraded piety of much post-

Tridentine Romanism has been taken over by some Anglican leaders and made by them a model and pattern for the Catholicism which the Anglican Communion maintains. Perhaps their mistake was understandable, because of liturgical and theological ignorance and ineptitude. But there is nothing to be said, today, for persisting in this error, especially when our Roman brethren themselves, in the throes of self-examination and self-accusation, are mending their ways.

Congregational participation in the liturgy is one of the significant aspects of the celebration of the Eucharist. This includes not only the communion of the faithful as a normal part of the action, but also full and intelligent sharing in the whole service, each member of the Body of Christ who is present at the liturgy taking his part, whether as celebrant or assistant, as server or singer, or as one of the congregation. The action of the celebrant is one in which each member of the Body of Christ is personally involved and personally represented. The Eucharist gives opportunity for external expression by appropriate responses, by common use of creed and chant, and by gesture and movement. When the whole congregation falls on its knees at the words in the Creed, 'who for us men, and for our salvation, came down from heaven . . . and was made man,' we have an expressive action in which the faithful realize their unity. Even such a simple movement as standing for the Gospel is part of the whole congregational participation in the Eucharist.

A member of the writer's family attended the Eucharist in a parish that prides itself on its 'simple service,' and also on its vigorous maintenance of a strong evangelical tradition. On his return from the service, he remarked, without realizing the strange significance of his words, 'That congregation is the most priest-ridden I have ever seen.' When asked why this was his impression, he explained that during the celebration of the Eucharist, there had been no layman in the sanctuary. Clergy alone had celebrated and assisted, without servers. The congregation had made no movement or gesture of any kind, beyond an occasional 'Amen' or mumbled response. His feeling had been that this was a rite performed for, but not by, the people. Yet even at a Roman Catholic High Mass in St. Patrick's Cathedral in New York, the congregation participates at least to the extent of standing, kneeling, genuflecting, bowing, making the sign of the Cross, responding to the bell at the 'words of institution,' and thus has some share in the action at the altar. St. Patrick's would be no model for the Anglican Church, nor indeed for the Roman Church as its liturgical revival would have it; yet the illustration has a point. The Catholic conception of the Eucharist demands, and must involve, such congregational participation as shall make the eucharistic action belong to the whole Body of Christ, focused at a given time and place.

The architectural setting for the pleading of the 'sacrifice of the death of Christ' is likewise not without its significance. Somebody has said that a church is an altar with a roof over it. Doubtless this is no adequate definition, but it is very suggestive. A Christian church is the place where the Memorial of Christ is offered—and since Christ gave himself in sacrifice, an altar table is the appropriate

central symbol of the Christian religion, architecturally
placed so that all eyes may be led to it. If there were nothing else to make it clear that Christianity is a religion built
about a sacrifice historically offered and continually pleaded,
the way in which the Christian Church came to build its
individual churches would be sufficient evidence.

There is one final point that requires brief attention. This is the relation of the offering of the Christian
Eucharist to the preaching of the Word. We do not wish
to leave in the reader's mind the idea that Christianity is sufficiently explained when it is called 'a cult religion.' That
it *is* a 'cult religion' is obvious, we believe; but there is more
to it than that. The preaching of the Word, which accom-
panies the sacrificial action, is an essential element in the
whole pattern and picture of the Eucharist. Most of the Anglican Prayer Books leave no doubt about this, ordering a
sermon at the celebration and making no provision for sermons at other services. Even in the American Episcopal
Church, where since 1928 a sermon is not *ordered*, the
Eucharistic Office is the rite where one is *indicated*.

Professor Whitehead, in *Religion in the Making*,
has said that the cult or ritual dance comes first in the history of religion. After that, he says, comes the myth that
explains the meaning of the cult. Now in Christianity this
is not the whole truth. For the 'myth'—by which we mean
here what Father Hebert has well called 'the Christian epic'
—historically comes first. The life and death and resurrection of Christ, with the meaning given by faith, come before
the cult action that celebrates them. This is true as a matter
of historic fact. But for the contemporary Christian, and

even for the interested outsider, knowledge of the event must be mediated by the community that centers its life in the cult. For ordinary purposes, the worship found in the Eucharist precedes the explanation of the meaning of that worship found in the preaching of the Word of God, by which the significance of the life in grace enjoyed by the Body of Christ is made plain.

This is another reason for deploring the tendency to separate 'mass for communion,' held at an early hour without sermon, from 'mass for worship,' held at a later hour with a sermon. The two belong together—or rather, the *three* do, for worship and communion and the hearing of the Gospel are all part of one single action. *Who* this is, *what* he does, *why* he does it, and who *we* are who receive and accept—this explanation of the Eucharist, with the corollaries that flow from it, should never be absent from the normal week-by-week participation of the faithful in the Christian Sacrifice. When the 'hearing of the Gospel' as it is preached in the church has been forgotten by the congregation, or when they have been deprived of it, there is great danger that Christianity may become nothing more than a refined 'mystery religion,' in which the historic set-ting, the whole life-situation, and the moral consequences of the action are lost. That Christianity is, in a real sense, a 'mystery religion' we have been prepared to allow. But it is a mystery that is historically grounded and factually based, with an extraordinarily rich range of meaning that goes far beyond anything that the ancient 'mysteries' could give. It is this side of Christianity, with its demands upon the believer, that the preaching of the Word is intended to safeguard. The worshipper must be confronted over and over again with the preaching of Christ—and of Christ crucified for the redemption of men—to the end that his participation in the eucharistic action may be intelligent and responsible, not merely formal and perhaps even superstitious.

Enough has been said in these pages to hint at the vast area of thought and suggestion that the actual setting of the Eucharist, its atmosphere and its manner of celebration, may offer to us. There is room here for all sorts and conditions of men, for all the arts and crafts they can bring, for the total dedication of life to God through the mediation of the pleading of Christ's redemptive work. Anyone who has long and faithfully taken his part and place in the Church's eucharistic action can have no doubt of its incredible richness, its wonderful variety, and its inexhaustible application to every situation and experience of man. This is what one might expect, for the natural expression of Christianity will possess richness and variety and unlimited applicability. The Eucharist, Paul Elmer More once wrote, is the only guarantee of the continuation of Christianity; perhaps that was too strong a statement, but it has its truth. In the Eucharist, the Christian Church's Sacrifice, the whole of Christian redemption is gathered up. Not only the thing itself, but the atmosphere and setting that like any ancient and traditional action it has generated, play their part in making it the heart of our religious practice and the highest privilege of which we are capable in this world of our human pilgrimage.

9] *The Eucharist in the World*

Our discussion of the Christian Sacrifice has so far been almost entirely concerned with its theological significance or meaning, its religious content, rather than with its meaning in the lives of the faithful who are members of the Body of Christ. This indeed was inevitable, since any further implications we may find in the sacrament will be based on the initial facts and the theological truths that are present in it. The Eucharist exists in its own right, not simply as a means to something else; its importance rests in the first instance upon what it is, what it derives from, and what it effects in the life of the Church. This truth has been well enunciated by Romano Guardini in his volume, *The Spirit of the Liturgy*, in which he insists that in eucharistic life as elsewhere *ethos* must be the consequence of *logos*— action must be the result of essence, 'doing' the result of 'being.'

On the other hand, failure to recognize that the action of the Christian Church in offering the eucharistic Memorial of the redemptive work of Christ has its inevitable implications in the wider life of the world has been responsible for some of the saddest chapters in Christian history. For it may appear to the spectator that the Eucharist is a private cult act, unrelated to the vast world of experience, and therefore irrelevant to men in their daily life and to the great affairs with which human society is concerned. And this is a perversion of the truth. We have already hinted at the way in which the life of the worshipper, and hence his work and the work of the world, are included in the offertory at the Eucharist. This is one part, but a vitally important one, of the relationship the Christian act of worship has to the life of the world, within which the Christian community lives and upon which it is to act.

We must protest against a misinterpretation found in not a few writers, of the Catholic idea of the relation of the Church to the world. Some appear to feel that when it is said that the first task of the Church is 'to be the Church,' this inevitably implies a disregard of the world and a willingness to let it go its way, without regard to Christian standards. Such a view is farthest from the minds of those who hold to the idea of the 'two cities'—one the City of God, of which the Church is an earnest; the other the City of Man, which is human society as it is organized for secular concerns. The Church has a profound interest in the world and it must bend its effort to conform that world to the justice that is of God. But while this must be done, the Church must also preserve its own integrity and identity. Here is no 'flight to the mountains' or 'movement back to the catacombs.' Here is a recognition of the truth that the Church is the spearhead of the order of supernatural charity placed in the midst of the order of relative justice, with the task of enabling men to live in the world so that they may be fit for God's charity. But they can never be prepared for this destiny unless this world is conformed, so far as in it

lies, to the divine purpose. Brotherhood and justice, peace
and freedom can be realized to some degree, in the here-
and-now.

As the Church has this relationship to the wider
world, so the Eucharist is related to that order. It does not
exist primarily to make the world better; it exists primarily
to be what it is—namely, 'the continual remembrance of the
sacrifice of the death of Christ and of the benefits which we
receive thereby.' But precisely because this is the case, it
implies the bringing of the entire world within the ambit
of that sacrifice. When it speaks of the communion of man
with his God, through the mediation of Christ in the Eucharist, it implies that the relationship there effected is to have
its reflection in such brotherhood with men, and such aid
to them in their search for their Creator, as shall make this
world a more just and more livable place. When it concerns
itself with the adoration of the risen humanity of Christ,
present through the instrumentality of bread and wine, it
implies that all natural things, the stuff that men grow and
make, the processes by which they do this, and the whole
creative activity of the human race are to be seen as related
to God and capable of reflecting him and his will.

Surely this priority of *logos* over *ethos* is justified
by the facts, historical and theological. It is the guarantee
that men shall escape frustration and despair from their
labors in the City of Man. For if the Christian sacrament
were solely to aid men in their struggle, it would provoke
them to desperation and misery, since its power would be
so ineffectually manifested in their daily doings. Because
the Eucharist sends them out to labor, but also gives them

the surety of an *is-ness* and a *givenness* of faith and life, wrought out in eucharistic action, it can indeed provide the dynamic that is necessary for social action, while it also offers some glimpse of their eternal destiny and provides some foothold upon the enduring realities that persist through time and change, through death and destruction. Sometimes our modern writers on the relation of worship to the life of the world need to remember that the much admired Society of Friends, with its tremendous contribution to society, finds in the high and holy hour of worship on 'First Day' the meaning of its religion—not because it is socially powerful, but because it is spiritually central.

The primary significance of the Christian Eucharist, so far as the organization of human life is concerned, is that the essential truth about things is vividly placarded before us. It is not so much that we worship at the Eucharist in order to be empowered for our daily life, to the end that we shall conform that life to the true pattern: it is primarily that all of life is to be lived in such a fashion, to be ordered in such a way, that we may more worthily worship at the Eucharist. *Then*, when we have sought to make an offering worthy of Christ, we can be empowered by him for fuller and more effective work in the world. Despite the activist trend in modern thought, we are prepared to insist that for the Christian the *telos* or end of life is worship and adoration. Man is made for contemplation, *theoria*, said Aristotle. And St. Thomas Aquinas, in defending an essentially Aristotelean position regarding the nature of man, maintained that the 'chief end of man' is the vision of God—worship, that is to say, at its highest and farthest reach. If this be so, it is a perversion to suggest that the Eucharist is only a sort of power house for social action, although it is quite correct to insist that the only adequate dynamic for Christian concern and labor in the world is the eucharistic offering of the Church and the holy food with which the faithful are fed. But this aspect of the sacrament is a by-product of the adoration of Christ's risen humanity, which brings God to us as we plead the redemptive work of our Head.

The two emphases in the Eucharist, which have an immediate social implication, are the *brotherhood* of man as the redeemed child of God, either potentially by creation, or actually by participation in the Body of Christ; and the *right ordering* of all things, upon which the liturgy is insistent in word and which it concretely manifests in fact. The underlying conviction behind both emphases is the reality of God's righteous will, and the necessity that man surrender himself to this will, so that it may 'be done on earth as it is in heaven.' Once man is the servant of the will of God, as a member of the Body of Christ, his obligation is to see in every other person a 'brother for whom Christ died,' and, seeing this, to live according to it. His social task is to strive for the proper ordering of human society so that it may reflect the pattern that is God's will, and consequently that it may conform more perfectly to the essential scheme proper to it, rather than remain 'in the evil one'—that is, in sinful defection from God.

Two criticisms have often been made of historic Catholic teaching about the 'world.' It has been charged that it is too *optimistic*, in that it appears to think that the world *can* be redeemed from 'the evil one,' at least to the extent that a sociological pattern can be devised and imposed on the world—a pattern that will be 'Christian' in its motivation and 'Christian' in its result. On the other hand, it has been charged that the Catholic tradition is too *pessimistic*, in that it appears to feel that the world is hopelessly inadequate, at best a sinful and frustrating sphere, and that man's true destiny is beyond the realm of the temporal, in eternity with God. Now these charges, while false, point to a truth. The Catholic tradition has insisted that the world can be bettered indefinitely, and in a Christian direction; and it has also insisted that the world, even at its best and when most christianly patterned, can never be the enduring abode of man, whose heart will be restless until finally it rests in God himself. The way in which the double criticism is made, however, is an indication of a misunderstanding of the genius of Catholic Christianity, as expressed signally in the eucharistic action.

If there were no possibility of some greater conformation of the world to God's will, the action of the Christian Sacrifice would be an absurdity, without relation to the total creation in which it occurs. The Christian Eucharist is a foretaste and intimation of the kingdom of heaven; to that degree it is the present experience of 'the perfect will of God.' The world order can approximate that consummation, never in the fullest degree, but yet increasingly as it is brought within the ambit of Christ's redeeming work. Men can realize their brotherhood, across race and class and color and sex and privilege, although the sinfulness that persists even among the redeemed will prevent the complete expression of their fraternity in Christ. They can strive, and with some success, for such ordering of human affairs as shall be more in accord with God's will: yet here, too, their sinful pretension and pride will interfere in such a fashion that at every level of ordering there will be the constant possibility and the inevitable presence of selfishness and power-seeking.

On the other hand, the Christian Eucharist has a deep eschatological strain. It has the motif, 'till he come . . .' This is the Pauline idiom for an insight that dominated early Christianity and has always been found in the Catholic tradition. The meaning of time is in eternity, and the goal of human life is beyond the limited here-and-now; while the direction of the temporal creation and of human living itself is toward some final consummation in which God will vindicate his creation, and man will see of the travail of his soul and be satisfied. This means, as we said above, that the Eucharist is foretaste and intimation of the vision of God for which man was created—there the Lamb is adored and the servants of God do him service. No sacraments or sacrifices are needed there, because the whole process of history is fulfilled and man, in redeemed brotherhood, beholds unveiled him whom veiled he adored in the days of his earthly pilgrimage.

This explains why the Catholic tradition has maintained that even the most nearly perfect social ordering, the most christianized pattern of human life possible in this world of temporal experience, is not sufficient for man's spirit. He requires more; he demands eternity, because God has set eternity in his heart and made him yearn for that complete fruition. The establishment of the most equitable social system, according to the principles of Christian moral law, will still not be enough for man. Nor will this kind of society, indeed, be established in its ideal perfection in this present world. The finitude of the world precludes total perfection. Not only because man is a sinner and, even when made a 'very member incorporate in the mystical Body' of Christ, still prone to self-seeking, but also because a created world is limited and partial, we are unable to envisage such a degree of supernaturalizing as would be required for society perfectly to express the will of God.

This position is not very different from that recently taken by Dr. Reinhold Niebuhr in his volume, *Discerning the Signs of the Times*. It is instructive that as Dr. Niebuhr has increasingly recognized the meaning of grace as power rather than merely as sign of favor, he has come to see the importance of a horizontal movement of God in history as well as the vertical movement, which alone seems significant for a thinker like Barth. He has also become more optimistic about the possibility of a more genuine christianizing of society, although he has not forgotten his earlier insistence on the imperfection and partiality of any such process.

Hence his point of view now approximates more closely the Catholic position of M. Jacques Maritain in his *L'Humanisme Intégrale*, where the relation of worship and social action is set forth along lines similar to those suggested in this chapter.

At the same time that we maintain this possible christianizing of society, we must not overlook inherent

limitations. To say that society can be christianized does
not mean that it will easily, or even with some slight effort,
become the City of God. The present human order of
things, as we interpret the meaning of that order, can *never*
become the City of God; that City is the order of supernatural charity, in which God reigns supreme and his will
is perfectly done in love. The Church which is the Body of
Christ is an adumbration and an earnest of supernatural
charity, although by reason of its 'incarnate' state it has its
empirical side, which prevents it from expressing in perfection its actual nature in divine intention and truth. But the
Church is not the world. The world, at its best, can become
more fully the City of Man, in which justice is the supreme
virtue, with human brotherhood and right ordering as its
manifestations. Even more than this is possible. Since Christians must live in the City of Man, they can bring their
supernatural charity into its midst and by that action 'in-
form' the justice of men so that it may become more nearly
the justice of God—a justice that in God's own being is
identified with his charity. But there is more. For it is of
the essence of the Catholic faith to say that the work of the
Eternal Word of God is also discovered outside the Church
empirically known in the world. Wherever men seek goodness, search for truth, and portray beauty, or in any other
way reach beyond themselves to that which abides through
all transiency and change, they are in touch with God himself in his self-expressive Word. Hence human society can
be the sphere for the most varied and rich manifestations
of God: manifestations that in many wonderful and unex-
pected ways suffuse the City of Man with the light of eter-

nity and give it a dignity and value that are beyond man's own achieving. But when all this has been said, it still remains true that the Church is the Church, the finite world the finite world, and the two can never be identified, although the Church can and must permeate and penetrate the world.

This is another way of asserting the peregrinal nature of man. He is a pilgrim, whose task is to live in this world as one who seeks a 'city that hath foundations, whose builder and maker is God.' He is not to disdain the path along which he walks; it has been made holy by the feet of God the Son, who did not hesitate to become one of those who tread this pilgrim way. The Christian is to do his utmost to make the path fit for those whom God the Son, by his redeeming Incarnation, has raised to be his brothers and potential 'partakers of the divine nature.' Above all, the Christian is to see that because he is a member of the Body of Christ, to which membership all men are called, he is fed with 'the bread of pilgrims,' and 'in the strength of this meat' he is to make his journey through the City of Man, bringing to it his new insight and understanding and working within it toward its highest possible perfection, while he keeps his heart still turned 'unto the mount of God.' There, beyond the tensions and frustrations of life in the City of Man, he will enjoy that which he can know only in part here below, even in the eucharistic action: 'the ineffable feast, where [God the Father] with the Son and the Holy Spirit, is to the holy ones true light, full satisfaction, everlasting joy, pleasure consummated, and perfect happiness.'

10] *The Eucharist in the Life of the Body of Christ*

In the preceding pages, we have discussed the important, not to say crucial, aspects of the Christian Sacrifice. Obviously our treatment has been inadequate, lacking in sufficient attention to detail, suggestive rather than conclusive. And yet it may be hoped that we have not left out of account any element of first importance; that all that has been said has been loyal to the Catholic tradition and has stated (perhaps 'in other words') what has always been regarded as essential to the peculiar action of Christian worship.

We have seen that any consideration of the Eucharist must be against the background of a theology that affirms that the Church is none other than the 'mystical Body of Christ, which is the blessed company of all faithful people.' The Eucharist requires faith in the Incarnation and in the Atonement as these are continued in the life of the Church—not as events of the distant past but as events that, through the Church as 'carrier of salvation,' are strictly contemporaneous with every generation of Christian history. Furthermore, we have asserted that the ministerial articulation of the Body of Christ, by reason of which a specific function has been assigned to a representative priesthood, is integral to the picture of Christian worship; although it is never sufficient—indeed, it is positively erroneous—to think that this ministerial priesthood is the sole agent in the worship of the Church. The laity—the people of God who share in Christ's royal priesthood by virtue of their being 'very members incorporate in the mystical Body'—are as much celebrants, although in a different sense, as the designated ministers of the sacrament.

After this, we made a survey of the New Testament evidence, coming to the conclusion that the Eucharist is a direct development from the Jewish table meals, but with the difference that it has become in Christianity the *anamnesis* or objective memorial of Christ's redemptive work, according to his words and actions at the Last Supper. With this in mind, we proceeded to consider other New Testament material and discovered that the Pauline and Johannine traditions are outgrowths of the events and practices recorded in the synoptic gospels—although in date of writing the Pauline documents precede the synoptic testimony, which has probably been considerably modified by later belief and practice. The experience of the early Church was next considered, and a brief survey indicated that the eucharistic *idea* as there presented is continuous with the New Testament material. Such development as took place tends to bring out more clearly certain central aspects of the rite without altering the direction established in the initial period.

Next, the eucharistic Memorial was shown to be primarily an Action, in which offertory, consecration, frac-

tion, and communion were essential elements. This notion
of action was examined to indicate that it is in agreement
with the general Christian conviction that God is known
chiefly through what he *does*, and that the supreme faith
of the Church is in the mighty act of God for man's redemption effected in the human life of Jesus Christ and that
which Christ wrought. A distinction was made between
memorial, in the modern sense, as mental reverie, and the
earlier idea of memorial, as action recalling from the past
and making truly present the event that is 'remembered.'
The Eucharist can be understood as a memorial in the latter
sense alone.

      This brought us to see that Christianity as the me-
morial of the passion of Christ is in a genuine sense a sacrificial action; the imperfect way in which this is presented
in various theories, some of which must be rejected as un-
congenial to the Christian spirit, does not preclude our
accepting the basic fact. It was suggested that the main
consideration here, as earlier, must be the nature of the
Church as the Body of Christ, dwelling both in the realm
of time, space, and unique happening, and also in the eternal realm where what occurs in the temporal world has its
abiding significance and finds its true consummation. The
Eucharist is the Christian Sacrifice, in that it is the pleading of that which our Lord did once for all on Calvary, and
the entrance into the significance of that event through the
identification of the Church as Body of Christ with the
offering of its Head.

      But since it is through Calvary that reconciliation

between God and man takes place and a new kind of fellowship is opened up between man and man, the Christian Sacrifice is also a communion. Here, through union with Christ, the faithful are brought by 'a new and living way' to their God, while in the common acceptance of salvation they discover brotherhood with their fellowmen at a level deeper than anything natural human community can offer. At the same time, the whole world, including nature itself, is brought back to God in principle, through identification with the offering of Christ; hence there is effected a communion even between nature and man, as there is between man and man, and God and man.

This communion in sacrifice is accomplished in Christ, who is present in the Eucharist after an unprecedented and unparalleled manner. So it was necessary to discuss the question of the nature of this presence. We concluded that Receptionism, Virtualism, and similar views denied the fundamental assertion of historic Christianity concerning the true presence of the Saviour in the eucharistic species of bread and wine, while Transubstantiation and Consubstantiation each had certain defects that made them impossible for us to accept. The most satisfactory theory to explain the indubitable fact of Christian eucharistic experience and faith was that we have a presence given in the species of bread and wine, in the sense that the risen humanity of Christ, which is continuous and identical with his human nature taken from the Blessed Mother, is brought to bear upon us through the bread and wine, acting as *organon* for this purpose. We concluded that the meaning of 'body' and 'blood' bears a relation to the belief in eucharistic concomitance and to the reality of Christ's risen humanity as hypostatically still at one with his deity.

We then turned to certain associated problems. First we sought to show that the setting for the Eucharist and the atmosphere it generates have become through the passage of the years intimately related with the action itself. They have the nature of 'significant form,' and are also a positive means of awakening a specific kind of sanctity, which may be called eucharistic and centrally Catholic. Finally, we concerned ourselves with the social implications of the Christian Sacrifice, pointing out the way in which the Eucharist both declares the goal for and provides the motivation toward social action, without suggesting that man's life and destiny are exhausted by what he does or can achieve in the world of time and space.

The summary we have just given will help us to see that it is no far-fetched statement to call the Eucharist the characteristic and significantly expressive action of the Christian tradition as Body of Christ. The Eucharist, as the Sacrifice that identifies Christianity, is Christianity at work in worship. It is the unique possession of the Christian Church, the unmistakable sign of its continuity and identity. It is not merely a sacrament in the commonly accepted sense of an outward and visible sign of *God's* reality; it is also a sacrament in the sense of being the external manifestation and operation of the inner reality of *the Church itself*—it is the sacrament of the Church as the Body of Christ.

In these closing pages, we would re-emphasize our conception of the Eucharist as characteristically expressing Christianity and the life of the Church as Christ's Body. We would reaffirm the truth that seems to us central to the entire discussion—namely, that without the Eucharist in the traditional sense in which it has been known, understood, and loved through the centuries, Christianity would be another religion. Efforts to secure a reunion of separated Christian bodies without due regard for the centrality of this sacrament, its sacrificial character, and its unique functions are both disloyal to the historic position of the Catholic Church and also a serious shift in the whole orientation of our religion.

It is often asked by good people, including those who consider themselves Christians, and who by affiliation are members of one or another denomination, what reason can be given for attendance at the services of the Church. Frequently the answers made to this question are sound enough, so far as they go, but quite unconvincing and inadequate. We may be told, for example, that every man needs, at least weekly, to spend some time in the consideration of spiritual matters; or we may be urged to support an institution that is necessary to the moral life of the community; or we may be informed that it is a needful discipline in developing a truly religious attitude to life. But all of these reasons, however true, are beside the point. For a Christian who understands the historic position of the Body of Christ, so far as its characteristic action in worship is concerned, they are quite inadequate.

The reason it is not simply desirable but utterly necessary for a Christian to attend not *a* church service but *one* specific service—the pleading of the Christian Sacrifice —is that historical Christianity is a religion that cannot be known and shared and understood without participation in its eucharistic action. To be a Christian *is* to be a eucharistic man; to be a Christian is to assist at the Christian Sacrifice. We have now learned—although far too many people have not yet grasped the point—that it is incorrect to call a man of good moral character, high ideals, and sound life a Christian unless he also accepts the historic faith. This is not to attack his good qualities, but simply to be clear on a matter of definition. We have also learned that the specific *differentia* in behavior belonging to the Christian man is a quality of life in which the sense of the supernatural, its reality and its pervasive action, is so apprehended that at least the beginnings of 'holiness' may be discerned in the believer. We are not content, these days, to say that the man who 'goes about doing good' is by that token a Christian, unless his 'activism' is based on a quality of life that, however dimly and inchoately, suggests the sanctity of the 'en-Christed man.' So also with worship. The test of Christian profession is not only one's belief in the faith proclaimed in the Nicene Creed, although it includes that. It is not only one's reflection of the supernatural charity and holiness of Christ, although it expects that, in however small a way, as a beginning in Christian living. It is also the acceptance of the plain obligation to be *of* the Church when it acts characteristically in offering the Passion of Christ to the Father, entering into communion with the risen Lord, and adoring him really present in the eucharistic bread and wine. This indeed is the external mark of a baptized Christian.

Now admittedly there will be a varying approximation to the full realization of this Christian profession. In the Body of Christ not every man holds the faith with the same firm conviction: in fact, each of us believes more surely at some moments than at others, while some of us are much of the time obliged to have faith in the faith of others, since our own lamp does not burn so brightly. Similarly, the degree to which we actualize the interior life in grace of the Christian Church, in our own behavior and in our own inner experience, will vary greatly, from person to person, from time to time. And in the same way, the members of the Body of Christ may not all of them realize as fully as they ought the essential obligation that is theirs as Christians to participate in the Christian Sacrifice. To a large extent this is because they have not been properly instructed by the clergy, who far too frequently have been derelict in their duty at this point. But failure to realize a fact does not abrogate the truth of the fact, or its necessity.

The Christian by his very nature is a 'eucharistic man.' As he lives *in* the faith, so he lives *by* the sacrament. As he is given at least the beginning of a life in relation to God through membership in the Body of Christ (and that is Christian salvation), so he is enabled to adore his crucified Saviour pleading before the Father the 'One Oblation' of which the Eucharist is 'the continual remembrance.' It is all of a piece. One can no more conceive a Christian life without the centrality of the eucharistic action in it than one can imagine a man who hopes to live healthily but refuses to take the nourishment that makes healthy life possible. To reject the Eucharist is in effect to reject Christianity itself. We must be fed by the life of him who is our Life. That feeding is in the Christian Sacrifice. To share in it is to know the life that is life eternal.

The ideal after which we ought to strive—or, even better, the reality we are to make actual—is perhaps best shown in a picture. Let us imagine a parish in which, through faithful preaching and pastoral care, the people have been brought to understand their vocation as Christians. Here each week the faithful will be seen coming to the church. The whole parish family will be gathered together round the altar, there to offer as a family the Holy Sacrifice and there to be fed with the 'bread which cometh down from heaven.' Instructed and informed by the sermon, which will make the *sense* of their common action a deeply understood and appreciated reality, they will yet be more vividly told of the meaning of their faith by the action itself: for this is Christianity really at work, visibly enacted before their eyes. Strengthened by the power of Christ, they will leave the altar but will not be without its influence at any moment of their workaday lives. There at the altar, as Christ's Sacrifice was pleaded, all of life—including their own—has been offered up to God; they are now sent forth to conform the world to God's holy will and to bring his supernatural charity into every situation in which they find themselves. The Eucharist is the renewed sign and seal of their membership in Christ's Body through baptism by 'water and the Spirit'; it is also their partial glimpse of their true *patria*, their 'bread for pilgrims', as they make their way through the world which God has created and which in Christ he has redeemed. Men they must remain, sinners they are—even if redeemed sinners. Yet they know that life has dignity and nobility, beyond its tragedy and frustration. They have had entrance into the mystery of the Cross, mystically represented and significantly present in the 'newer rite.' Their Christian profession comes alive as they visibly demonstrate it by their assistance at the Church's Sacrifice; and as they go forth, with 'the peace of God that passeth all understanding' in their hearts, they go forth 'in the strength of that meat' which is given for their Christian living in this present world.

Nor is this just a picture, an imagined thing. Day by day, week by week, millions of men and women and children find precisely this in the faithful following of the eucharistic way. As we have said, not all realize it in perfection—few, if any, do that. But in all races, among all peoples, through every range of ability and talent, for every type and condition of men, the Eucharist has proved itself for what it is. Pragmatic tests alone are not conclusive, but neither are they to be despised. Long-range results, rich and fruitful lives, deepened and deepening understanding, true piety, heightened courage, a sense of meaning and direction for living, and above all increased awareness of God and sensitivity toward other creatures: these are valuable evidence when we are considering what the Eucharist is and what is signifies in the Christian tradition. The kind of religion that is built upon this sacrificial-sacramental action is Christianity as history testifies to it, with its blending of awestruck adoration of God and grateful communion with him; of austere discipline and humane morality; of divine authority and human freedom. The unutterable majesty of the Father, 'of purer eyes than to behold iniquity,' is coupled with the profound self-giving of God, 'who for us men and for our salvation came down from heaven . . . and was *en-manned*' in the person of the Eternal Son; while the moving Spirit 'who with the Father and the Son together is worshipped and glorified' works everlastingly to make us free men, daring to address our God as 'Father' and enabled to live, even here, as brethren who are members one of another in Christ. This, we say, *is* Christianity; and this is the eucharistic mystery at which we assist and by which we live.

George Tyrrell once remarked that Christianity is the Eucharist and charity. That is not all; for he forgot to add that the charity with which Christians are concerned is the charity of God brought to earth in Christ and his saints, while the Eucharist depends upon the faith that this charity is none other than God himself. Yet in effect he spoke the truth. For the Eucharist contains and expresses all of the Christian faith, while its inevitable consequence in life, for those who know its true significance, is the charity that is the chief 'fruit of our redemption.'

So the Eucharist in the life of the Body of Christ is nothing other than that Life which is the life of the Body

—it is Christ himself, offering and giving and loving. It is Christ's action, as it is his sacrifice and his communion and his presence, shared with those who by virtue of their membership in the Body are one with him. 'I am that living bread which came down from heaven; if any man eat of this bread he shall live forever: and the bread that I will give is my flesh, which I will give for the life of the world . . . He that eateth my flesh, and drinketh my blood, dwelleth in me, and I in him . . . As the living Father hath sent me, and I live by the Father; so he that eateth me, even he shall live by me. This is that bread which came down from heaven: not as your fathers did eat manna, and are dead: he that eateth of this bread shall live forever.' So the Johannine writer represents Christ's eucharistic gift.

One of the great paintings of the Flemish School is the Adoration of the Lamb, by Jan van Eyck. The whole company of the blessed, taken from all walks of life, and joined by the heavenly host, are gathered in worship of the Lamb slain for the sins of the world. All creation, including in it inanimate nature as well as man and the animal world, seems united in the great act of adoration. The presence of the Lamb suffuses the whole scene with a supernatural light and brings into a single fellowship all who are bound together by their common participation in Christ. It is a portrayal of the Church in its eucharistic action. This artistic representation has moved a modern Christian to give us a hymn that states, better than we could hope to do, the meaning of the Christian Sacrifice in the life of the Body of Christ:

The Church of God a kingdom is,
    Where Christ in power doth reign,
Where spirits yearn, till seen in bliss
    Their Lord shall come again.

Glad companies of saints possess
    This Church below, above;
And God's perpetual calm doth bless
    Their paradise of love.

An altar stands within the shrine
    Whereon, once sacrificed,
Is set, immaculate, divine,
    The Lamb of God, the Christ.

There rich and poor, from countless lands,
    Praise Christ on mystic rood;
There multitudes reach forth their hands
    To take God's holy food.

There pure life-giving streams o'erflow
    The sower's garden-ground;
And faith and hope fair blossoms show,
    And fruits of love abound.

O King, O Christ, this endless grace
    To us and all men bring:
To see the vision of thy face
    In joy, O Christ, Our King.*

L. B. C. L. MUIRHEAD

* From the *English Hymnal*, by permission of the Oxford University Press.